18 Wheels and Bill

VI and Bruce
To our good friends and nutty
ones. Hope you have a Great Life
from your other nutty friends
Juanita and Bill —
2011

Juanita Gill-Schoen

authorHOUSE®

AuthorHouse™
1663 Liberty Drive
Bloomington, IN 47403
www.authorhouse.com
Phone: 1-800-839-8640

First published by AuthorHouse   4/19/2011

ISBN: 978-1-4567-4607-0 (sc)
ISBN: 978-1-4567-4608-7 (hc)
ISBN: 978-1-4567-4606-3 (e)

Library of Congress Control Number: 2011907670

Printed in the United States of America

Forward

The things I have written about in this book started when we first went back on the road. Writing was one of the things that made the trips worth it. So much to see and do and I thought perhaps there was someone else who might be interested in what our country is really like.

I thank Bill and God that I was able to see so much of it before our economy got so bad.

I never thought I would see the day when our elected officials would try to take our precious freedom from us.

I don't think we'll let them.

18 WHEELS AND BILL

They pulled out of the truck stops, waysides, service plazas, red, blue, any color imaginable. There long sleek bodies attached to long orange, white and yellow trailers, forty eight to fifty feet long and then there's your twenty and thirty-two foot pups.

But it's those long forty eight to fifty three footers that will grab your attention. Like the flatbeds that sometimes have a full load on them covered with special tarps of maroon, green, blue, etc., that catch the eye.

If you watch these men that drive these trucks, they fasten down their loads and pull the load straps tight to keep their loads from shifting and keep the tarps in place so they stay dry. You can almost see the muscles pop out. Their work is taken seriously.

The men are not necessarily six foot tall but the average would be five six or five eleven. Some big around and others thin but with muscles to show for their work. Even the Ladies get in on the joy of truck driving as a team or singly and most of them are darn good.

Bill likes to chit chat with the men and women on the CB and has some pretty good conversations with most of them. When the language starts to get a little raw he shuts them down.

Rolling down the highways, sometimes singly, but a lot of times eight or nine or more make up a group of truckers we like to call a convoy. It's quite interesting to listen to the bunch of truckers carry on a conversation between them without someone cutting in.

Bill and I always thought it was great when we joined a convoy.

Sitting high above the four wheelers we look down on them to see that they look so vulnerable. The truckers try to be courteous to them but it is

1

difficult sometimes. Especially when they squeeze in front of the trucker and he has to put on his brakes to keep from running over them.

The small cars are cursed by the big trucks and the big trucks are cursed by the small cars.

If it weren't for the people in the smaller vehicles who make or package the products or produce, there wouldn't be the need for the men and women who drive the semi have to haul the products and produce.

We must be courteous to each other, or at least try. The truckers watch out for each other. They warn of the smokies or black and whites or whatever color they are that are knocking at their back door or others who are pretty well hid. Giving credit to most of our police protection and highway patrol doing their duty, they sit out in plain sight letting us know that they are out there trying to keep the accidents down for the semis and the smaller vehicles.

Listening to the old timers with some thirty, forty years of driving experience behind them like Bill, the young drivers of today could learn a lot about respect on the road. It use to be that a person had to be at least twenty five years old to drive a big rig. From the looks and actions of some of these young drivers, you would think they were still in kindergarten. Some of the language that comes out of their mouths when they are talking on the CB and goes out over the air waves is terrible and should not be allowed. Why doesn't the FCC do something about it?

It doesn't hardly seem fair that when a trucker is at rest after a long day, why then is it that an officer will knock at his truck door at a service plaza or a rest area and wake him up to see his log book. These truckers are trying to make a living like everyone else.

They're required to rest after so many hours of driving and so they do not need the hassle of these officers. There are inspection stations for this. However if an officer is using this to make a check on someone who might be a little shady, then he is only doing his duty. So much of a driver's time is spent fighting road construction delays, people getting out of work, accidents, and delays in loading and unloading.

Finding the right streets in a strange city can be very frustrating. Weather, toll gates and waiting forever at a truck stop for their food can take away precious time these men and women do not have.

So many people do not realize what a truck driver's job entails. It use to be that a truck driver was treated with respect. He would be one of the first ones to be served at a restaurant. Truckers use to be a proud people.

Clothes were clean, not looking like they could stand alone or like they had been worn for a month without having been washed.

You could step outside your truck without having to hold your nose because there are some who are just too damn lazy to walk a few feet to the truck building to pee. Disgusting you bet. I admire the ones who take the time to really clean themselves up. These are the ones you can really be proud of. It shows their pride in their work.

There is no reason a driver should look like a bum. There are a few drivers who really do have some dirty jobs and I can make allowances for them. And there are drivers who work for companies whose trucks are really dirty inside and so they don't care what they look like on the job. Bill always made sure his truck was clean before he left the company's yard with it or when he was ready to give it up. After all, it was our home for many months.

To my way of thinking, every truck driver should be made to clean their truck before leaving it for someone else to use. We have seen trucks with two to three dogs or cats in them.

Imagine the smell or damage to these trucks. These trucks should be inspected every time these drivers come into the yard. What an expense to these companies. We really wonder what these peoples' homes look like.

Three cheers for an officer who arrests a driver who has been drinking. Rather it's a four wheeler or a semi driver. A young man seen coming out of a tavern walked toward his truck and got in with every intention of driving off when an officer saw him and stopped him. Needless to say the young man was furious because he felt the officer had caused him to lose a few days of work. He was still talking about it a few weeks later on the CB. The officer didn't cause him to lose time, but his own stupidity in thinking he could drink and drive. The officer did his job.

This trucker would have had between thirty and eighty thousand pounds of a lethal weapon in his hands and some innocent person or persons could have been his victim. Or he could have been his own.

Truck stops and service plazas are a haven for a driver who needs to get off those long ribbons of highways. As anyone who sits in front of a computer all day can tell you, the eyes get tired of the constant concentration and can do funny things to your eyes.

Most truck stops are clean and have good service and food. The buffets are okay but they are a repeat day after day and you do get tired of them. You really long for some good old mom and dad cooking. But if you're in a hurry, buffets are the way to go unless you're watching your dollars.

Bill and I carried a large cooler with us and kept cold cuts, bread, soda, water and a few other things in it. Manys the time we didn't have time to stop and eat, so I would fix a sandwich for us. As they say 'Without Trucks, America stops' so we must keep moving to get our products to their destination on time.

Most truck stops are quite accommodating with showers, diesel fuels, service garages, lounges, chapels, laundry and stores. It is seldom that a trucker will carry much cash on their person. Lot lizards, whores, and transits that come begging can't expect much of a handout. It doesn't pay to carry money on you. There have been stabbings, killings, and beatings because someone thought a trucker had lots of money on them. Trucking is a scary and a lonely job and I believe that is why a few do have a guard dog with them. That woman's or man's truck becomes that dog's possession and you sure don't want to bother it.

We see so many beautiful and strange sights as we travel these thousands of miles of highways. Bill and I discuss what we see and I try to put it on paper for future reference.

Like the beautiful mountains we go over. The water rushes down the sides of Mount Eagle making the rock formations shiny and looking slippery. The road is steep with a six percent grade and we hit a speed of thirty miles per hour with our heavy load. Some drivers take the risk of going faster. But no matter how many miles Bill has on him, he always believes in safety first. At one time, a driver passed us with a smoking tire. 'Hot brakes.' Runaway ramps are placed at strategic locations in case a driver gets into trouble.

Bill has never tried to follow another driver down the mountain. You never know what is at the bottom. So he always does what he feels is best for us.

We have missed being in so many accidents or seeing them happen because of a stop for a lunch break or taking our dog for a walk. Just something that kept us from being there.

Our dog Prudence was our pride and joy. She was a miniature schnauzer and as smart as could be. She was Bill's dog but I soon lay claim to her too. If she strayed too far, all Bill had to do was clap his hands and she came back to him. If she got upset with us because she couldn't have her way, she would turn her back on us and pout.

She loved steak, and one night when bill and I were in a restaurant eating, a waitress delivering a large steak to another customer behind us had her tray tip and spill the steak on the floor near us. We asked her what she was going to do with it and she said throw it out. We asked her if we could have it for our dog. Prudence ate from that steak for three days. She sure was a happy dog. But she still had her pouting times.

Bill likes to tell of the time she was on the bed and she wanted a drink of water. 'Woof' she would go. If I didn't pay attention to her, she would go 'woof', 'woof' again. Well then I would pick up her bowl of water and hold it for her while she had her drink. Spoiled? Yes. But we really loved her.

Accidents we've seen have included drivers who were over tired and tried to keep going to make their pickups or drops on time. Some are real bad where the big trucks are tipped over and their sides and tops are ripped open and everything is spread around. Sometimes the driver is killed, but a lot of times they are just hurt and can walk away from it.

Travel trailers in a hurry are sometimes seen lying on their sides in a ditch. We've seen cars and vans reduced to accordion size because they were in a hurry or you get a nasty tempered driver who thinks everyone should move over for him or her.

Well that's enough complaining, though I could do more, but would it do any good?

Look at us, were a big long heavy machine. Traveling down the highway at sixty five miles per hour. We've got eighteen wheels rolling, carrying freight to every state in the United States.

You name it, we got it. Were up before the crack of dawn, not even sure if we got all our clothes on. Eyes aren't wide open just yet, but get us a cup of good hot coffee and we sit up a little straighter and talk a little louder as other buddies join in the conversations.

But we haven't got long to chit chat so we end our tales of the day before. Some stories are long, some are short, and some quite amusing and I wish I could remember them all.

With a wink of an eye and a bill paid too, were on our way once again to start our day.

The roads are long and rough and the old CB is crackling, warning us of what's at our back or front door. Alligators on the road, blown truck tires, four wheelers stalled on the side, accidents, and many other obstacles that happen throughout the day.

Then someone strikes up a lively conversation clearing the last of the sleep out of our eyes and our bodies. We stretch and yawn and take a sip of the hot coffee we brought along and can finally taste it. 'mmmmm'.

We blow our nose and clear our sinus. The air is dry in the bunks at night but you don't leave your windows down or your doors unlocked.

You can't trust the people that come around truck stops or rest areas all hours of the night.

You try not to park near a cattle truck. The smell or the stomping of the many cattle in the trailers can drive you batty as you try to sleep. Now reefers, that's a different story. Their noisy but you can tune them out. Bill has a problem with doing that since he's very sensitive to noises.

In the early morning, the engines hum as those big wheelers get ready for their runs. Fuel time, breakfast time, or just good ole caffeine time. A bag of chips, a few candy bars, a gallon of water and a couple of sodas to see us on our way.

If it weren't for the big trucks where would America be? As the slogan goes, "Without Trucks, America stops."

Those little fiber glass cars going seventy five miles an hour seem to float over the highways at that speed and I wonder if their tires even touch the ground. I'm one firm believer that if that speed were cut down to sixty or sixty five miles an hour for those light cars there may be fewer accidents. The cars are too light and speed too fast.

It seems like the cars are getting smaller as they're trying to get better gas mileage. But those cars don't have a chance if they get hit. They crumple like an accordion and the people in them do not usually survive the impact. But I guess that is one way of lowering the population. Even with the air bags, these people are not safe in these small cars.

When I see these small vehicles weave in and out between semis and other traffic I hold my breath. The chances they take aren't worth their life or their children's. But that's exactly what they pay with. It's really heart breaking when we see this as we travel these long highways. Setting the speed at fifty five for truckers hurt business and truckers. Most of the truckers are professional drivers and have thousands of miles behind them, on all kinds of roads and weather.

After we dropped our trailer in St. Paul, Minnesota and waited for one to be loaded, we bobtailed it to Raymond street to the old Key Restaurant. Bill had first eaten at it in nineteen- seventy-three when it was first started by Barbra and Roy Hunn and has now turned the business into seven restaurants. They are located throughout St. Paul and run by their children. It was a pleasure to sit in the high backed polished wooden booths which still had the coat hangers on them. We sat down and ordered our meal and before we knew it, our food was in front of us and delicious.

There are no fancy dishes here, just great tasting food. Nothing much has changed but the prices and the cash register. The small bathrooms still have the old twenty inch doors and the old tin molded ceilings.

Another sight that was interesting to see was the long accordion type busses that bend easily around corners as they carried passengers to and fro.

We left St. Paul and encountered some pretty rough roads between there and into Iowa. Bill adjusts the trailer axles and that helps. There's a beautiful sky to my right as the sun prepares to set. The bright pink of the sky feathers out and the smoke from some factory flows into the air and becomes a pink spiral.

We come upon the tall grass prairie reservation near Strong City and the Flint Hills that Jessica St. James talks about in her book "Show down at Sin Creek". That is a good book and if you want a good laugh, read it.

In the distance there are tall white wind mills turning to help with the electric shortages. The land is flat and you can see a long way in any direction and we spot a few oil wells.

This is farming country and there are large granaries along the highways. It is unbelievable as we approach the end of January and there is no snow to speak of. It makes you wonder about the farmers and their crops.

We stop at Mead, Kansas for fuel. The home of the Dalton Gang Hideout. I think it would have been very interesting to have toured it. But you don't get off the beaten path when you have products to deliver.

Just a few of the other trucks on the highway are HO Wolding, Werner, Fed X, Koehl, Jim Palmer, Roadway, and many others. Depending in what part of the country we are in.

There are many Schneider, Yellow, Swift, Wall-Marts, J.B hunt, and many, many more. When we see these big travel trailers going down the road pulling another trailer behind them and sometimes a boat behind that. We wonder where the highway patrol is, especially when they're almost as long as a semi. We wonder if they have to have a CDL or special license to do this or can they get away with it. It really doesn't seem fair if they don't. That really seems more dangerous than a semi.

A few years ago, we heard a story of a man and woman driving down the road in their motor home. She was driving and the man told his wife he was going to put it on cruise because was tired and wanted to take a nap. "All you have to do," he explained to her, "is steer it." The man went and laid down. After awhile, the woman thought she would make a sandwich as long as the motor home was on cruise and would do its own steering.

7

Next thing she knew they were in the ditch. I don't know if they got hurt, but I think she learned a valuable lesson.

We saw many motor homes and fifth wheels on the roads. It's a shame these people that drive them do not have to take a driver's course before getting behind the wheel. What little experience they get when buying one of these and driving one around the block is not enough for them to qualify to get out on the road with one. I repeat, a CDL should be required.

They should also have to go through a weigh station for their own safety. Some of them probably have more on than is allowed by law. We learned the hard way also. We've been there, done that and seen the results.

We travel across Kansas which is as wide open as Missouri and they just sort of flow into one another. Liberal, Kansas has many large beef feed lots and we see many semis waiting for a load of cattle. Liberal is quite a town with large granaries, restaurants, and motels, if you would like to spend some time there.

You can buy many of the Wizard of Oz figures there. I really enjoy that movie. When our children were growing up we watched the movie with them whenever it was on. Guess what, I still watch it when I can. Judy garland was great.

Back in Oklahoma again, farmland spread out as far as we can see. What beautiful country. Here I go, getting nostalgic again over a movie. But Skuda Hoo Skuda Hay was another of my favorite movies with Jane Powell and Roddy Mcdowell. They don't make movies like that anymore.

There are pyramids of Milo and stacks and stacks of hay. Coming out of Dalhart, Texas there is one continuous feeding yard after another on both sides of fifty four west, and what a smell. Whooee! But you gotta raise the beef somewhere. And that beef is American raised.

A few cattle truck drivers were overheard talking about a driver who was standing by his truck in a truck stop talking to another driver when something hit him in the face. "My God" he swore, "what was that?" He rubbed his hand over his face and swore again as he wiped cow shit off his face. The other driver hooted and said you never stand too close to a truck loaded with cattle.

Just a few more miles and we were in Santa Rosa, New Mexico and will take time to shower and eat and relax a few minutes and walk Prudence. We are back in adobe homes and hill country. I love the styles of the adobe homes. They're so unique and pretty.

The Guadalupe Mountains are to my right as we travel down the highway. Deep ravines and dried up streams are many. Some homesteaders have taken up residence on the desert, and some RV'rs can be seen at the foot of the mountains.

About thirty eight miles from Flagstaff there is an advertisement of the Historical Meteor Crater, which we cannot see from the road. There are rocks placed in such a position as they look like picnic tables. Flagstaff has snow on it but the roads are clear and we have a beautiful sky and sunshine.

Geronimo camping grounds can also be found in Arizona.

There is elk country, but for as many times as we have gone over flagstaff we have never seen one. There are mines here for red decorative rocks. There are many historical sites to be taken in.

The speed limit is sixty five and we can make good time and the big wheels are rolling. We reach the peak of Flagstaff which is seven thousand thirty five feet above sea level. We follow forty west to the bottom. There are high rock walls and the Grand Canyon is far off to the right at exit one sixty five on sixty four north.

We are at a six percent down hill grade and can see for miles in any direction. What a sight. The roads are smooth black top but hard to see on a black, rainy night with headlights coming at you. At the bottom of Flagstaff we come into Kingman.

We level off for awhile and then climb again. Our ears pop and we yawn a lot. But what a magnificent view. We are still at five thousand feet and there are signs of ranches off in the distance as cattle roam over many acres.

Far, far below us we see other big rigs going up while we are heading down. Where the mountains have been cut through for the highway it is like going through a roofless tunnel. Bridges criss cross the roads and high line wires stretch every which way for miles. We watch as trains loaded with products disappear into long tunnels and come out again on the other side.

We are running low on diesel fuel so we stop at a fuel island to fill up, adjust the trailer axles for California loads and pound the tires to make sure they have enough air in them. Los Angeles is three hundred forty five miles from Kingman.

Mountains and deserts are the normal scenery again. But the view of the mountain is ever different.

We cross the Colorado river and stop for an inspection station. They check out Bill's log book to make sure it is up to date and to keep track of what is being hauled in and out of their state. The long stretch of desert sand looks hard packed but we watched about a dozen motorbikes riding off across it and they sure kicked up the dust.

Bill and I were heading for Deming, New Mexico from Albuquerque a few months ago and ran into a dust storm and we could hardly see. To make matters worse, it rained. What a muddy mess we had.

Traffic is heavy as we once again head for Los Angeles and we crawl along. It is very hazy and the mountains are in shadow. The wind has picked up as well. We drive on Dale Evans and Roy Rogers drive and pass the museum in Victoryville. It is raining hard and the sky is dark. Looks like it will last awhile.

Traveling on, we come into San Bernardino National Forest and head down highway fifteen to ninety one to Carson and our drop. What a view coming down.

In the distance is what looks like a silver ribbon of highway with the light shining on the wet road. A runaway ramp heavy with gravel lays off to the side.

We're unloaded at Carson and find some place to park for the night and go to bed as it is late. We sleep most of the next day waiting for a load.

The city maps in the atlas help a great deal to find our destination in the big cities. Thank goodness for them.

Calumet and Scandia playgrounds look inviting but we don't have time to play now.

At the TA, there is absolutely no place to park but the big rigs keep pulling in and out hoping someone will leave.

Bridges, bridges, bridges. Oh what tangled webs we weave when to construct bridges we do conceive. It seems no matter where we look they are building new ones.

Once again we are in the San Bernardinos in California and the clouds hang dark and heavy. It looks like rain again. The wind has come up more but we are settled for the night and won't have to fight it. Bill and I are small town people and would not want to live out here unless we had a chauffeur who knew just where to go when we wanted to go.

There are trains heard where we are parked for the night. While I love the sound of them rolling down the tracks and their whistles, Bill doesn't sleep too well with their 'noise' as he calls it. It's music to my ears though and has been since I was a child.

In the morning we are giving our orders again for our next pickup and drop. We play the game of red light, green light and again yellow. Though it takes awhile to get through them in the big cities, thank goodness for them.

Back through LA we go to Montebello for our pickup and then head for Denver, Colorado for our delivery.

It's amazing the things a trucker hauls all over the United States. Did you ever stop to think about how you get those products you use on a daily basis? We've hauled beer from La Cross to Springboro, Ohio. Rolls of plastic from Tomah, Wisconsin to Griffin, Georgia. Quick creamer from Wisconsin Rapids, Wisconsin to Flanders, New Jersey. Powdered milk from Philadelphia to Wausau, Wisconsin. Bird seed from Saint Louis, Missouri to Menominee, Wisconsin. Shelving racks from Houston, Texas to Charlotte, North Carolina. Flat glass from Mooresville, North Carolina to Tomah, Wisconsin. Bent sheet metal from Saint Paul, Minnesota to Phoenix, Arizona. Etc, Etc.

At Independence, Missouri we drove into a limestone underground cave to pick up tires. Although it was scary for me, it was a sight I'll never forget. It was very huge and so white. It was a wonder none of the trucks took any of the large pillars down that held up the ceilings. The pillars and the cave was so fascinating.

We drove about one half to three quarters of a mile in. There were offices, docks, storage and places that were being carved out for what looked like more storage. Security was tight. My one thought when we entered these caves was that this must be something like what Osama Bin Ladin and his terrorist's caves must look like. But not as clean and probably more web intersected.

It's an experience to be a trucker and see so much. There is so much more to see off the highway, so we make a list of places we would like to see with the family. Places inaccessible with the truck.

Highway six o five north is heavy with traffic. I love the tall palm trees and the tall sky scrapers, but give me the three story buildings, that's high enough for me.

I look down from the high bridges we must go over and my stomach does flip flops, but the view is fantastic. When you are below the high bridges, it looks like the big trucks are leaning toward you.

Bill explained that the centrifugal force will carry the truck to the outside of a curve and it will make the truck corner easier. It helps maintain a steadier speed. It's seldom that we have a load shift as we travel. The products are generally loaded so they won't move.

Things are a little slow for the truckers until about the fifteenth of February. We are a few of the lucky ones as the company and brokers keep us moving.

The ships bring products to America for the trains to deliver to warehouses. Ain't that a slap in the face for America! Have you noticed how many businesses you go into that are run by foreigners? What has happened to our beloved America?

In a tourist town in Wisconsin, where the population more than triples from June to September, I went to seven motels looking for summer work. I was told they only hire their own people out of Chicago. These were all foreign owned businesses. If you don't know the rest of the story you might ask Paul Harvey, Jr. or Rush Limbaugh.

There is plenty of snow on the San Bernadino higher peaks. The sun shines on it as the clouds move away and brings out the shapes of them. Hundreds of wind mills are turning in the wind at the foot of these mountains, generating electricity for miles.

A little further down the highway we pass the Gene Autry trail. Gene and John Wayne were two of my favorite actors. They sure don't make them like those two anymore, nor can Hollywood make a decent movie. They think violence and sex are what the people want now days. The horror movies are so bad that when I catch a view of them they make me want to throw up. Even the cartoons they make for children are terrible. There are few that I would want my grandchildren to watch. Because again there is sex and violence. Isn't there anyone who can make a decent movie or cartoon anymore?

We travel on the Sonny Bono Memorial Highway that is strewn with litter which isn't unusual to see traveling across America. We give credit to the states that do a good job. We know it must be really hard to keep our roadsides clear with the millions of people who use them and thousands of them who just don't give a damn. Don't you just wonder what their house or yard looks like?

We are now in the high country climbing slowly. We are carrying a lot of weight so Bill keeps the speed down. Bill has driven for over thirty five years and he says you never follow another man off the mountain.

There are rest areas, and trucks and cars a like use them. In the summer time they are especially full with tourists.

Entering Arizona we go through their Port of Entry and show the I.F.T.A. Wisconsin registration cab card and International registration card and are on our way. We enter the Palen and Chuckwalla Mountain range. Boondockers are stretched out across the dessert as far as the eye can see. It's a cheap way to enjoy the warm weather but it's a good idea to have a generator or several florescent or battery operated lights unless you go to bed early or sit around a campfire. A blue boy is also handy to have to empty your septic in.

January twenty ninth. Heading over Flagstaff again we picked up the first snowfall and we've been pretty much in it for quite awhile and it isn't getting any better as we head for Gallup on snow covered roads. The road crews have been out sanding and that helps.

We are in Navajo country and again the rock formations are unique. We are passing the yellow horse tourist attraction again. The snow is coming harder and the roads are getting bad again. There has been one car flipped over ahead of us and a big rig slid into the ditch. Thankfully no one was hurt as we are flagged on. The scene before us is beautiful but hazardous.

The weeks have flown by and we are now into February. We are seeing a lot more snow. Seems like it doesn't know how to stop. We stop at the Port of Entry to get a permit to travel into New Mexico. At the TA just down the road, we pull in to make some phone calls to the company and the Broker. The truck stop is packed with people just trying to get a few minutes break from fighting the snowy roads.

The sun is trying to come out as we head over Grants Pass. The roads are no better but the scene is truly a winter wonderland. Traffic is getting heavier, more so going west than east on forty. Heading north on twenty five we have run into some terribly bad weather and roads. Our speed is minimal as it is snowing so hard we can hardly see and the wiper blades keep freezing up. We have to stop every few miles to clean off the wiper blades and the windshield.

We finally pull into a truck stop and sigh with relief. We call Port of entry and they tell us Raton is ice packed and slippery. We stay where we are until morning. We eat breakfast and are on our way over icy roads and over Raton. Thank God there have been salt trucks out ahead of us.

The day is clear and cool and the sun is like a fire ball. A few truckers and an Americano bus kick up snow and slush as they pass. Heading up and over Raton, we hit more bad weather and roads. We have our four ways on and are moving about twenty five miles an hour. Two other trucks pass but we are going downhill and are heavily loaded.

Coming into Colorado at the top of Raton, we slow even more trying to get off safely.

Today we know "God is our copilot". Thank you GOD! We finally make it to the New Mexico, Colorado weigh station. There are a few hardy Rivers trying to get somewhere. There are quite a few stores here, including a Wal-Mart which we pull into and restock our large cooler with groceries and go on our way.

The Great Sand Dunes are out here in the San Luis Valley. With all the snow I would have to call them the Great Snow Dunes. It would be great skiing and snow mobile weather.

Pikes Peak International raceway is just outside of Pueblo. There is lots of snow on the Pike. The smoke from a power plant goes straight up. An old saying is "when smoke is high, we'll have blue skies. When smoke is low, we'll have snow". The Mantou Cliff dwellings are near Fountain. There is some snow but the roads are clear.

Church towers point skyward and it's the old ones that fascinate us. We are in Denver, "The mile high city" at five thousand two hundred and eighty feet above sea level. Denver's Technological systems are there. It is a large business. Invesco Field "the playground of the Denver Broncos is on twenty five north and a large amusement park is nearby.

We pick up seventy east to our destination for our drop. We have a web of bridges and manufacturing Industries all around us. It looks like manufacturing boulevard. After our drop in Denver we head for Loveland. The snow is heavy on the higher elevations. We have been over five thousand feet most of this trip.

At Loveland we phone some relatives and have them meet us at Mc Donalds. We have a great visit and enjoy the children.

Leaving them, we pick up shelving to take to Beiley, Michigan. We arrived at approximately three P.M. and didn't get loaded until two A.M. We are quite often early with our drops or pickups and we know we have to wait at times. We stayed at Fort Morgan and slept.

Blue skies and sunshine woke us. Roads are good and there is no snow at all. Our fuel gauge is wacky and has been ever since we got the truck. But Bill has figured it out as to when he needs fuel again. We get about twelve hundred miles out of two hundred gallons.

We are in corn country and the rolling hills of Nebraska. There are large farms scattered throughout the land and a few large beef ranches are seen here and there. We eat breakfast at Julesburg, Nebraska and head on down the road and fuel at Total on highway eighty east. Truckers pull in and out at a steady stream and at Bosselman truck center. They sure need more places to park trucks from Loveland to Julesburg. The parking situation is critical all across the United States.

We are finally caught up to our own time zone, just a few miles out of North Platte. About thirty miles out of Kearney, Nebraska we come across a stretch of road where a big rig lay on its side and another was just being righted. Cars and trucks left their tracks where they went in the ditch one after the other without waiting for a number.

Further down the road we stop at a small family owned restaurant to eat a lunch. In a corner booth, an elderly trucker sat. His voice carried and I listened intently as he rambled on about putting the hammer down or how he had to beware of the bear sitting a mile down the road.

"What was he talking about?" I wondered with interest. His voice wrapped around me as I listened on. Then I knew as others started talking, telling their special stories. He had been a trucker for forty five years. You could see the pride in his face as he talked.

"I was married to that eighteen wheeler." he declared. "I was twenty five years old when I hopped into my first one and I knew then it was all I'd ever want to do."

"What about getting married?" someone asked. "Didn't you hear what I just said?" grinned the old man. "I married that truck the day I climbed into it. I named her Lucy Ann and she took care of me for many years. Then of course there was Lucy Bell, Lucy Jean, and last was Lucy Marie."
"Why did you name them all Lucy?" asked a young driver.

"When I christened my first truck Lucy, I meant her to be the only one I ever had. Young as I was, I thought she would last forever and when I finally had to trade her in for a new one, I knew it would always be Lucy I was married to."

"But didn't you ever want a real marriage, with children and a home to go to when you had time off the truck?" asked another driver?

"No," he answered. "I knew I would never be able to give them the time and attention they would need and want. I knew a lot of truckers who had all that and lost it because they were hardly ever home. They were out there trying to make a living, to give his family the best he could. But it wasn't enough for them. The money was good and it took care of the wife and kids. But when half of the union is missing most of the time it can become disastrous. I didn't want that kind of heartache.

Though Lucy would get stubborn and balk at times and let me know I had to pay attention to her, she was always a pleasure to be with. Oh I wasn't always alone with Lucy, I had my share of the real thing, but I never committed myself to any of them."

"One in every port then?" Terry replied knowingly.

"Yes and no," replied the old man whose name they had learned was Jim. "There was a red head whom I fell in love with and took on my trips for three years. She was a real honey. She knew from the first day I met her that I would not marry her or anyone else. One day when I stopped to pick her up after being apart for two weeks, she just wasn't there. She was gone and all her things with her. I never got that interested in another gal again.

Guess I couldn't blame her though. She wanted what I couldn't give her."

"Sorry old man." one of the truckers said.

"Naw. No need for that. I chose my kind of life and I haven't regretted it. If I took time off it was to go see my folks or brothers and sister. But after a week away from my Lucy, I was always glad to get back to her."

On I-eighty in Iowa, we stopped at the world's largest truck stop. What a truck stop! It had everything a trucker could want. Restaurants, clothing, reading materials, game rooms and a lounge where a person could relax, watch TV or just visit. Showers, laundry and much more was provided for the comfort of the drivers of the big trucks.

We crossed the Mississippi River just out of Colona, Illinois on eighty east. Traffic has become heavier and lots of big wheels rolling.

We head for Holland, Michigan, home of the large Tulip Festival. The ground is covered with snow. It is only one fifteen but it looks like five or six o'clock in the evening. As we cross the Kalamazoo River the roads are as bumpy as ever.

We stop at Tulip City truck stop. We're only thirty miles from our drop at Beiley. We stay at our drop over night and the wind rocks the trailer all night. Thank goodness we are loaded.

The plows have been out and the main roads are good as we head north on thirty one to Manistee, Michigan for a load of sand. You just never know what you're going to have on next.

There isn't much to see of Michigan out here on thirty one and it's a dismal, dreary day falling over the snow covered land. It is snowing at Ludington and the roads are rough with snow. We finally arrive at our pick up destination. We are hauling sand. A special blend to be taken to Texas, our next drop.

We ate our first meal of the day around three and stopped at Sawyer to fuel up. The sky doesn't look good for Indiana. The truckers are pulling in to fuel up and to find a place to park for the night. But at five o'clock the truck stop is just about full. We travel to Mattoon and bed down for the night after Bill catches up his log book for the day. He is very diligent about making it come out right.

Traveling down interstate fifty seven south we have a smoky at our front door and another at our back door. But they don't bother us. The eighteen wheelers are rolling again after a night's sleep, fueling and breakfast. Some of the truckers buy snacks and coffee or soda to help see them through the day.

We are still having bad weather and the windshields are hard to keep clean. Salt and dirt kicked up by other passing trucks or trucks in front of you can really mess up a truck. Fed X and Steel Case that are usually quite clean take their share of the dirt also.

Some trucks that are privately owned depict beautiful designs and scenes such as "Old Icy Blue" and their "New Icy Blue," which is owned by Harvey and Karen. The inside of the truck is fantastic. Go to a truck show if you want to see how proud these truckers are and what a great job they do with them.

We go through Arkansas and miss a lot of what it has to see. The Passion Play it puts on a couple of times a year, Eureka Springs and the country music places that have been built there and so much more.

The fields are wet and bare. Some are as green as new spring hay and then there are those old cotton fields that haven't been plowed under yet.

We go up and over the muddy Arkansas River and head for Little Rock. About ninety miles from Texarkana it is starting to snow and the farther we go the worse it is getting. It is wet and heavy.

We pull into Normans Forty four at Prescott, Arkansas, fuel up, eat supper, walk the dog and head on down the road, hopping to put on a few more miles before retiring the truck for the night.

At our drop in Arlington, they unload us at seven thirty. We are getting milled magnesium hydroxide powder (sand). It is used as fireproof material in dry walls and some plastics. We turn the corner from our drop and there is a Six Flag recreation area and not far from there a General Motors plant.

Later in the day we stop at a William's truck stop. We've always liked the service at them but at this one, you either eat from the smorgasbord or you order from the cook. There is no waitress. A trucker likes a little pampering after hard hours of driving and they want the food hot and now.

Fast foods are fine now and then but not all that often. So many truck stops have gone to fast foods because they can't get waitresses and I can't say as I blame the waitresses for not wanting to do this sort of work when they can't get decent wages or tips. They shouldn't have to depend on tips. People get the wrong ideas that a trucker can afford to leave a tip every time he eats in a restaurant or a truck stop .

We pull out of Williams Truck stop and go on down the road to Flying J where we sit down and have a friendly waitress in a minute and our breakfast in ten.

We head out of Dallas on I twenty west. We leave the snow behind the closer we get to Louisiana but the skies are overcast and we expect rain anytime. We pull into a Seventy Six truck stop and park it for the night as we have no orders for the next day.

We play a few games of five hundred rummy. I won the first game but Bill won the next. He most always wins. After I taught him how to play Hand and foot he started beating me at that too. Guess I showed him too many of my tricks. While we have a little time to waste, we visit with a niece of mine and her family who live nearby. We let the children sit in the truck so they could see what it looks like inside. It was a big thrill for them.

When we got our call for our pick up in Shreveport. We said our good-byes and were soon there. There are several trucks there already but it doesn't take long and three of us are loaded with rolled felt roofing and on our way as others come to take our place.

Heading out, we take highway three. God, what a road! The grooves catch the wheels and bounce us around. Have you ever looked down the road and seen where the wheels of the big trucks go?

Now entering Arkansas once again we have roads that are a little better. There is a lot of swamp land and I think of the history of the large plantations and the colored people who lived under the conditions that still exist today along highway three and twenty nine.

President Clinton must have known about it as he only lived about thirty five miles away from there in his childhood. I calculate his hometown of Hope to be that far away. How about it Governor, don't our own people deserve a look. It seems the other people that come to our country get better treatment than our own American born. We so eagerly and freely give them a hand out of homes, gas stations, motels, medical assistance and welfare while because we make a dollar too much our people are turned down for any kind of help. What a farce!

How about our wage scale? Shouldn't it be at least nine dollars an hour. With the prices going up, it's hard to keep up with them, especially when raising a family, paying for a home, sending the children off to college, etc, etc. Talking about raises, how about the Social Security being raised to at least five percent each year and go up according to national prices so the senior citizens can keep up with their medical prices and rent. Of course the problem with the rent is every time the seniors get a raise in Social Security the land lords take a good chunk out of it.

Whoever thought up the saying, "The Golden years", were off their rocker. There is no such thing as the Golden years. Now if we were a Senator or Congressman we could vote ourselves a raise every year and not just a three or five percent. And we could go on vacation and have a great time.

So many poor people, so little money, so little help for America's poor and older generation and sick and disabled. What's happened to our proud country "America". We see so much of our loss as we travel across the U.S.A. "Yes, we the truckers feel it too." What would the world do without trucks? We discuss this and a lot of other every day happenings between ourselves and with other truckers who feel the same or at least have their opinions on the same things and we get downright ornery about the economy and the way it's going.

From twenty nine north we pick up thirty east. Arkansas got more snow and I'm sure they need the moisture.

Jumping Gees, this road makes you feel like you're going to land back in the trailer.

I heard once that a truck drivers insides can be rearranged and I believe it after traveling on some of the worst roads there are across the U.S.A. Many are being rebuilt but there are so many of them in such bad shape and not enough money for the states to do the work that needs to be done.

We came upon a bad accident where a tractor trailer has gone off the road and is totaled. A little farther, two cars have gone over the embankment. We get a little squeamish when we see these things but it doesn't matter how good a driver you are, these things happen.

A truck driver coming past the accident told how he laid one over on the driver's side. He had his seat belt on and because he did it messed him up good. Another driver told of laying his over on the passenger side and if he would have had his seat belt on he would have been crushed. You figure it out.

A little slush, some ice, a broker giving a driver a thousand mile pick up or delivery ten o'clock on Tuesday and want you at your destination by three on Wednesday the next day. When does this driver eat or sleep and what about traffic backups, accidents, bad weather and speed limits? These all have to be figured in, in a trucker's route. I wonder how many of these brokers have actually driven a truck and gone through a day like this? Those brokers don't pay the tickets out of their pockets.

These men and women who put their lives on the line day after day to haul products to keep America running, deserve more respect than they get. Isn't it time to bring back the courtesy to them, to those who deserve it? Really!

Tow trucks are trying to right a Fed X truck tipped on its side in a ditch on I forty. We usually don't find out just why some accidents happen but can pretty much speculate on why it happened.

We travel across Arkansas, Missouri, and Illinois and into Wisconsin where we sleep and drop our load and then go to Milwaukee to pick up another load.

We have two days off to go home to take care of business and see the family. We have a grill out, though it is a little on the cool side, but we enjoy it.

We have two drops on Monday morning. One in Arcadia and one in Rochester, Minnesota. There isn't much snow the further we go but the hills in the distance are covered with snow. Some of the hills are covered with broken trees. Looks like wind damage. They add to the scene as they lay dark upon the hills. We cross the old steel bridge that brings us across the Mississippi.

Just out of Winona we pick up more snow. The roads are so bumpy on forty three and ninety. It's worse than sitting in a vibrating chair that's gone haywire. We head for ST. Paul for another load and it is so windy, we watch the birds being wind driven as they catch the currents and go with it. Bill fights the wind and we finally get over the bridge.

Change of plans, so we go back through Winona and on through Galesville to catch fifty four which is rough, crooked and wet. First time we've been over it and the last. It seemed a shorter route to Marshfield, Wisconsin, but because of the sharp curves and roughness it takes us longer.

We get our first pickup in Marshfield and head back to St. Paul,

Minnesota, for our second pickup. It didn't make since to go all the way to Marshfield, Wisconsin and then have to go back to Minnesota when we weren't that far from St. Paul. It's hard to figure these brokers out, especially when we were expected in California on Thursday. But we didn't complain too much as the more miles we put on, the better for us, I think.

Our drive back to Minnesota is a tiring one as Bill fights the wind again. It is very strong as we drive on the open highway. Our destination was changed from St. Paul to Burnsville, Minnesota. The city lights are glorious in their colors before us, as they light up the city.

We fuel up, catch the log book up, walk the dog "Prudence" and have breakfast at Flying J Truck stop in Des Moines, Iowa. We grab a jug of water and head out across thirty five south. There is very little snow and we have a very beautiful day. The wind has finally let up. Traffic isn't bad and the big rigs are rolling. Our speed is sixty five and we could use another five.

We watch a nice looking long haired dog dash across in front of us at a high rate of speed, across a ditch, up and over a barbed wire fence. At the rate of speed he was going, something either scared him or it was supper time and he sure wasn't going to miss that.

We are rolling down thirty five east, the same road we traveled two years ago and the highway was so bad with ice and snow you had to take a number to get in the ditch. Today it's as clear and dry as ever. The weather pattern sure seems to be changing and that means changes for farmers and many others. If only they can get the moisture they need.

Traffic is getting heavy as we near Kansas City, Missouri. We find smokies all over the place. There is a lot of construction going on but traffic is moving smoothly. Rolls of large cables sit along the highways waiting to be shot through a pipe to connect up with other cables eventually. Fiber optics. What's the world coming to?

We enter the weigh and inspection station and are waved on.

Have you ever noticed the old telephone poles that still sit along the highway and how they look like crosses and do they remind you of what our Lord died upon for us? It's sad to see that reminder but I believe we need that more than ever today. We have a tendency to leave God out of our lives.

To the southwest of us the sky is a glorious pink to lavender. It looks like God has taken his hand and swept it along the skyline. I try to capture some of it on my camera, but it is never as beautiful as the real thing. In the distance the trees stand in dark contrast. The oil rigs bob their heads as if in slumber.

Another beautiful day across New Mexico and the sun brings out the colors in the rocky hillsides. Each time we come across this hilly and scrub infested land we notice something different. More color in the hillsides, old ruins half buried in the distance or different rock formations. Rusted car frames of the nineteen thirties or older sit in gullies also half buried. I wonder what other treasures can be found out there on that vast dessert along highway forty west.

A mile long train sits with empty flatbeds while a railroad crew works beside it. Another group of men and women keeping America rolling.

We stop in Santa Rosa to fuel and shower. Aaah! We do this as much as possible. Sometimes it's a stretch between stops, but we carry wet ones with us for just such occasions.

Thinking about the crews of people who keep America working, there are so many of them. Our Policemen who try to keep us safe, our Firemen, rescue workers, pilots, doctors, nurses, the different branches of the Military, construction workers, teachers, factory workers and of course the men and women who drive these large semis to bring the products where ever they are needed and so many more. We are all out here to make a living, To keep America going.

We are going over the Sandia, Gallup and Flagstaff Mountains. I love the mountains with the ever changing scenery and the valleys far below. It's a long hard pull and I still get a little squeamish when I look down at the scene below. But I can't resist the view.

Albuquerque, what a city. The tan and blue web of bridges that criss cross the highways reach far above us. Cement abutments are placed on one side of us and ten foot walls on the other. Homes high on the hills look down on it all. It makes a person wonder how they get up there.

Dune buggies have been busy as they race across the sand feeling the power of their machines and the wind. What a thrill! The colorful range of hills a few miles out of Albuquerque could be called another badlands. They stretch for miles. Volcanic rock, black as coal, lay along either side of the road as we near Grant, New Mexico.

We stop at Milan, New Mexico at the Petro Truck Stop. Smorgasbord is good but expensive. Prices have gone up all over and we would fix lunch in the truck but without much room it is hard to do.

Gallup, here we come once again but under better conditions. The Red Rock State Park is a gorgeous site against the blue sky. Fort Courage is another tourist attraction worth seeing, don't miss it if you go to New Mexico or Arizona. It is on forty west, right on the New Mexico, Arizona border. There are Indian ruins just up the road from Fort Courage. We are over the Gallup Mountain range and on top of Flagstaff. It is seven thousand three hundred and thirty five feet in elevation. We have about one hundred and eighty six miles to the California border which is at the bottom.

The breakfast and service at Petro was good at Kingman, Arizona. Our drop is at Rancho St. Margarito on Friday.

Today is Valentine's Day and a young man just gave his wife or friend some roses. He got a kiss for it.

We picked up a nail in a rear tire and it has been leaking air for several days. Today Goodyear is fixing it for us.

After we leave Goodyear and head forty west we see to our right more rock formations. If we glance up we see what looks like a kneeling Nun. Just down from her another one is seen with several people kneeling in front of her. The imagination is a great thing.

We pass over the Colorado River. The water is so green and smooth it looks like emerald glass.

We are about fifty miles from Laughlin but we don't make the detours to go there as we have a drop to make somewhere else. Laughlin is a cool place to gamble.

We go over Providence Mountains toward Barstow, California and then over Cajun Summit or Bernadino National Forrest at an elevation of forty two hundred feet. Each mountain range stands higher than the other. Holy cow, what a view! I have never seen a view like this. We were over these before but it was raining so hard we could only concentrate on the road. The valley is far below us and a long train pulls and pushes it's load uphill and around curves. Traffic is heavy and it is windy and warm, about sixty five degree. School busses are finishing their runs for the day.

Coming out of Rancho St. Margarito on two forty one north we have bumper to bumper traffic on six lanes of traffic all ways. It is like Christmas lights spread out before us. It is a circle design where the roads intertwine from other lanes and ramps. All that was missing was the blue lights spread out amongst the red and white and it would have looked like the American Flag.

We pick up our next load at Fontana, California. We heard it's called the city of Industry. Trucks, trucks, trucks. So many in one place. Motor homes by the dozen are rolling. Two motor cycle police men roll up beside us and then turn off on a ramp. There are mountains again bathed in a shadowy mist and reaching majestically toward the sky. There are large wind generators turning in the breeze like a graceful ballerina along the Sonny Bono road.

Heading toward Tucson on east ten we come through a tunnel and under a web of bridges. It is Friday and traffic is heavy on this day February fifteen, two thousand two.

February sixteen. We stopped in Deming, New Mexico to visit some friends and had breakfast with them. The town hadn't changed much but they did build a Wal-Mart store right next to the K-Mart store and put a fence between them with a gate.

On our way back to Wisconsin we cross the St. Francis River. It looks so cold this morning, I don't think I'll go for a swim in it. It is very windy and much cooler as we get to Wisconsin. We stop to eat and Bill makes his calls and sends his faxes.

Our waitress is an elderly woman, older than what you normally see waiting on people in a restaurant. She could hardly get around. She explained to us she needed the money to pay for her medicines. What a shame! You raise your family, work and save for retirement expecting to enjoy life at least by the time your seventy. But then you get sick and it zaps everything and more than you saved. How about it Mr. President, couldn't you give the elderly of these wonderful Golden Years a little more of a raise each year to sort of match your raises you and congress and the Senate vote yourselves?

We finally get back to Wisconsin and a few days off for a eightieth Birthday celebration. My brother Carl still enjoys fishing, puttering around in his garage and a little dancing now and then. We had a great time.

We leave Tomah after a short Cesena plane ride. What a view at three hundred feet up. I'd love to go up again, it's like you're standing still and yet you see so much. The cranberry bogs, the layout of the town, the Veterans Hospital, Wyethville and so much, more. It's quite a town.

We travel to Brooklyn Park, Minnesota and drop our load. We go on to Shakopee, Minnesota to pick up a load of shingles and we wait, and wait, and wait. We had a nine thirty appointment and got loaded at one o'clock. There were many trucks ahead of us and many behind and still more coming in. Everyone is fit to be tied, it was a chaotic mess. You don't make any money playing a sitting game. We head for the scales to weigh up and wait again to leave the yard, which is finally at two o'clock. We head for La Cross, Wisconsin and stop at Cannon Falls for our first meal of the day.

There are a few flurries and the weather does get bad. We have blowing and drifting snow all the way back to Thoma. We sit in the yard from Monday until Thursday. The load we were suppose to pick up Tuesday wouldn't be ready until Wednesday and then it became Thursday before we could leave. We got a different load Thursday to take to Rhinelander from Hammond and then we came back to the yard. Our load for California is finally ready.

We ate breakfast at the Veterans Tribute Restaurant at Cadot.

What a great tribute to our men and women who have and are serving our country to protect her shores, our skies and our people. Traffic has become less as Old Mother Nature is working her wintry blast across Iowa. It is the last day of February, Two thousand two.

It looks like March is coming in like a Lion. As we travel further, the snow has turned to rain and then back to snow again.

We stop at Emporia for the night. It hasn't been much fun fighting the wind and snow packed roads.

Morning finds us joining the other traffic again until we stop at Newton, Kansas to fuel up both the truck and our selves. We still have bad roads and it is windy on top of it all. A motor home has gone into the ditch and lays on its side. An eighteen wheeler is in the opposite ditch but the driver managed to keep the truck up right and a small four wheeler is laying on its top This time no one got hurt. About twenty miles out of Pratt we have clear roads again and blue skies. But it is still windy.

We call our family in Wisconsin and they have eight inches of snow. The snow plows have been busy throughout the night, plowing and salting to keep America moving. Thanks Guys!

A large herd of cattle are seen circled in a bunch with heads facing into the wind. They are snow covered and look cold. But I am told their thick hides keep them quite warm. Probably to a point.

The green fields we saw across Kansas a month ago are now frozen and white. Thank goodness it is March, in which case Spring can't be too far behind. Can it?

Part of Oklahoma is still windy but not as bad as it has been. Texas had a spotting of snow as we first came into it. But with a temperature of twenty four degrees it is cool and fairly calm. The big feed lots are as full as ever. Where's the beef? Right there in Big T.

We stop at Nara Vista to eat. It's a quaint little restaurant, clean, good food and good service.

There is something about the morning when you watch the sun come up and lighten up the day for all of God's creation and man's. Take time to look at the plowed fields the farmers have so diligently worked up in the spring to get ready for their crops. Look at the green fields next to them. Have you ever noticed the contrast? The beauty of it? Maybe that's what makes a true farmer. They can see it.

The trees leafing, the flowers coming out to bloom and the tiny plants coming up through the earth that has been made ready for them. It sheds a new light on everything and makes you feel good about yourself and things around you. As the saying goes 'It's a great life if you don't weaken.' It really is. Just look at the beauty God has given us. If only every one could enjoy it and take it for what it is. A gift.

At Barstow we stop for the night and have very delicious ice cream sundaes. We stay overnight and have breakfast. The breakfast would have been good but it was so cold in the restaurant. We had to wear our heavy winter jackets and our food got cold before we could finish it. Sorry Rip, it's a beautiful place you had there but turn up the heat a bit.

Back on the road again and rolling with the other big wheelers. There are a lot of us this morning heading for LA. Rolling over the San Bernadinos again the traffic is very heavy. Going south on fifteen, the ranges ahead of us are very heavy with mist and there is some snow on the higher peaks.

An accident at the ten split is slowing traffic and causing a major back up. It is rush hour and what a time for an accident. But we encounter a lot of them and it's all part of the job.

Next we head for Lompac, California. We take ten east, five north and one thirty four west to 101. We see the famous ABC building, the Disney building and film studio where they are making a movie on the back lot.

We see acres and acres of strawberry beds as we head on down the highway. We travel out of Oxnard north along the Pacific Ocean where the water looks so green. There are many oil derricks to be seen. From a distance they look like huge ships. Along the roadways there are ice plants in bloom. They are what we call Moss Roses in Wisconsin. There are various other plants in bloom of which I do not know the name.

We are so hemmed in by buildings and trees it feels like a tunnel. We go through a beautiful part of Santa Barbra and it is very busy and crowded and very cool. We are still traveling along the Pacific and the water is much bluer. Looking at the huge body of water you wonder how there could be such a shortage of water.

As we leave the Ocean drive we enter Mariposa Valley on north 101 and come into a great scene! These are places I have only read about and dreamed about until now. We go over Santa Ynez mountains and go west on two forty six.

Coming back along the Columbia River going east on eighty four were in what seems like a wind tunnel. A car trailer "or known to the truckers as a parking lot" is being tossed from side to side. It's rather scary as sometimes coming over a mountain there is nothing on either side of you.

We watch the mighty white capped river as the wind draws the water from it spraying it high into the air like a sheet.

The ducks take up residence on it and on the few small Islands that are scattered here and there.

White caps add cottony color as they dance along with the waves. We catch a glimpse of Mount Hood peeking over the vast hillsides covered in a blanket of snow.

Crossing over to highway fourteen we cross the Port of Hood toll Bridge. Too scary for my blood. I never want to cross it again, but I may.

We are on the Washington side again with about the same view as Oregon. We are going down the main street of Bingen, Washington.

A heavily loaded train rumbles along side of us and the mighty Columbia.

The water is deep and the river is wide and a deep blue green and free of pollution. May civilization never touch it.

We can but imagine the trek of Lewis and Clarke through these many ranges along the river. What a hardship it must have been.

The Dallas Dam stretches across the Columbia near the Goldendale aluminum Company and the Columbia continues its run to the great Pacific Ocean at Astoria.

New Mexico, Two thousand two, November Seventh.

Coming across forty going west the clay ground is a reddish color and the highway ahead of us looks like there have been many people and animals killed and their blood has bled into the black top as a grim reminder to drive carefully.

Heading toward Los Angeles on fifteen south an odor penetrated the air that had us covering our noses to keep from gagging. We thought it could be some of the large cattle ranches but it smelled more like sulfur.

We dropped our load at Buena Park and went onto Ontario to pick up another load. An appointment for three o'clock turned into an hour and a half wait which wasn't bad.

The lights of the city really show up in the darkness of the night and we have miles and miles of red tail lights and white head lights. The decorative lights of some of the big rigs really show them off.

CB's are being used and a woman tells of a horse she'd trained and one day when she was riding it, something spooked it. She went up and he went up and it was a good thing she wasn't a virgin because when she came down and hit the saddle, she wouldn't have been anymore.

Another story told was about Burt Reynolds coming down the Golden Stairs and meeting the Pope going up.

"I'm going to see the Virgin Mary." Said the Pope.

Burt smiled at him and said, "She ain't no more."

Often we run with a good bunch of men and women and sometimes conversations get a little glitzy but usually it's intelligent and you can learn something new, no matter how old you are.

They say you are not old if you can learn something new every day.

We like running the Southwest because it seems to be cleaner and we're not hearing the Cadillac Man every three to five minutes telling about his tours to Mexico, and telling the truckers they can get two free beers and a bottle of Tequila.

A lot of us wish he would take that stuff and drown himself in it. We don't need any more drunks on the road.

There were several men who took him up on the deal and went with him on the tour and he left them stranded in Mexico and they had trouble getting home. But they took care of him when they got back to the United States and he wasn't on the CB for quite awhile.

Another sore spot with the truckers are the prostitutes that hang around the truck stops or the rest areas. There are also the Yard Lizards who come around begging for money.

At Ontario, California we pulled into a TA truck stop for breakfast and there were Police cars and an area roped off.

A drug dealer had been shot and killed just before we got there. Thank God we missed that.

We're heading for Flagstaff and the clouds are dark and threatening. We never know what the weather will be up there.

The transients are still out begging for food or money. I can't call them all homeless because we have seen them at the end of the day head for and go into a house or a rundown motel.

Stopping at a small town in New Mexico for a couple of days waiting for some orders, we watched a young woman standing on a corner holding up a sign.

The first day it read "I'm pregnant, need money to get home."

The second day a young man and two dogs joined her and she held a sign that read "need food, were hungry, God bless."

When we left on the third morning she was alone holding another sign, dressed in a heavy warm coat and a nice pair of brown boots.

We've heard stories how rich some of these transients really are.

We'll give to the food pantries, Salvation Army or Goodwill where these people can go and pick up these things for nothing.

A lot of these cardboard holders look as capable of working as you or I. I'll grant you there are some who really do need a hand out because they are afraid to go to these places because of an illness or being mistreated.

A few years ago a close young friend of ours needed help badly. He lost his job and home after his unemployment ran out. He tried other jobs but because of his health problem - border line attention deficit - he would have anxiety attacks, panic attacks and couldn't stand to be around a bunch of people.

He needed help badly and we took him to Social Services and they said they couldn't help him because he didn't have a home or children or a job.

Well Hells Bells, he wouldn't have needed their help if he had.

We didn't know what to do and his parents lived in another state and didn't have the means to help him either.

After trying to commit suicide several times he finally got the help he needed. It took about five years but with the proper medication and the right people working with him he is doing alright.

At Holbrook, Arizona we stop to fuel. The wind is so strong it makes our trailer rock and turns the air brown.

There is a beautiful multicolored rainbow over the red rocks near Gallup, New Mexico. Always something new to see as we spot another.

It's good to be up at daybreak and watch God's magnificent hand sweep the sky in all its glory and color. We are traveling across fifty four east in Texas and what a glorious sky at sunrise.

It's Sunday morning and I'm reminded of Johnny Cash's song "Sunday Morning Coming Down".

The clouds now go from cottony white to silver grey with a touch of pink threaded through them to a metallic blue to a dirty grey. What a wondrous sight to behold.

Bill and I make out different forms in the clouds to pass the time going across the long, almost uninhabited prairie. Cattle by the thousands graze here and large granaries stand along the road way.

As you awaken to a new day you know the Lord is out there.

Tanya Tuckers song is probably about as good as it gets when she sings "When I die I may not go to heaven, cause I don't know if they let cowgirls in. But if they don't, just bury me in Texas, 'cause Texas is as close as I'll get".

We see a face in a silvery white cloud that reminds us of Jesus. Neither happy nor sad but looking down on his world reminding us he's here for us all.

Sometimes on a clear blue sky day, there will be light feathery clouds stretched out that we like to call Angel Wings. There is beauty wherever you look if you want to find it.

It is Christmas from Wisconsin to Texas to all over the World. Santa Claus in his colorful outfit sits in many front yards as we travel down the highways. Strings of lights of every color brighten the yards, eves of roofs and the trees.

Statues of deer made of wire with lights bob their heads as we pass by.

Colorful displays of Santa and his Reindeer sit on roof tops delighting children as they fantasize Santa flying with a sleigh full of toys.

Red ribbons brighten many trees of homes as well as the many bulbs glistening through the windows. Light Christmas music comes from our radio and makes everything more festive. Restaurants in truck stops are gaily decorated which helps to remind us that the Holidays are coming up.

Isn't it great the joy that is shared. The smiles and the gifts that are so happily given. Even if there are no gifts, it's the whole idea of family gathering together to celebrate this great Holiday.

Why can't the joy of friendship be carried over?

Driving through Wyoming, Iowa was a beautiful sight. Homes were decorated and above us the most glorious arch of red and green as we entered the town.

We gazed in awe at it because we hadn't seen anything quite like it in years. Almost every house had candles in their windows.

At Dubuque another amazing sight greeted us. So many lights and decorations.

When we saw the beautiful decorations at Abilene, I felt like a child again. I use to think there was nothing more fantastic than the Fourth of July fireworks. But they don't last for long and I sure look forward to them every summer.

To me Christmas is the most powerful and beautiful time of the year.

Traveling across eighty four we saw hundreds of brown winged geese crossing the blue sky looking for a place to land for food and water.

Further on we saw several flocks of Snow Geese with their shiny under bellies gleaming in the sun. What an awesome sight.

Entering New Mexico on eighty seven west the sky was black with Geese again.

We are almost alone on this long stretch of highway where there is hardly anything to see as we head for Raton Mountain pass. Snow has been coming down but not enough to bother us going over.

We rest at Petro for the night in Laramie, Wyoming after hitting icy highways and high winds.

We have a light load of seven thousand pounds of plastic articles. Monday, December sixteen, we are traveling over the Rocky Mountains through Elk Pass. The deeply grooved roads do not help with the high winds as we are being pushed sideways.

There is snow on the hills around us but the roads are clear. The sand trucks have been out and as other semi-trucks pass us, they kick it up and our just cleaned windshield is mud spattered and stone pitted.

Across Idaho we have some snow and then some rain.

As we hit the Oregon border the speed drops to fifty five miles an hour. We are in wide open spaces and hardly any traffic so it seems strange not to be able to travel faster.

Cruising over the Blue Mountains we have a magnificent scene. We have hills all around us once again and a glorious scene ahead of us.

We can see for miles and we follow the Snake River for several miles. Maybe in our next life I'll be a woman "Daniel Boone" and Bill will be Daniel Boone and we'll explore the rivers, mountains and canyon.

Close to Baker City we cross the forty fifth parallel, half way between the Equator and the North Pole.

Our drop is in Hermiston, Oregon at a Wall-Mart distribution place and the appointment is for five o'clock in the morning.

31

But they have four hours to unload you so you sit and sit until they decide to get around to you. Actually you could sit until twelve or one o'clock. Is it any wonder drivers get pissed off? You don't make money sitting and there are a few others I could mention. It really gets to you. Beware! You'll sit.

Traveling north on seventeen we are looking through fog as thick as pea soup. Bill turns east on I seventy to Worden for our pick up of vegetable seeds. The weeds and grasses are thick with frost making a wintry scene.

About thirty miles out of Billings, Montana going west on highway ninety we see an unusual sight that is seldom seen anymore.

A pick up with several bales of hay was headed east and a large herd of cattle were following it with a 'tall in the saddle' Cowboy, all in black, was bringing up the rear.

I rolled the window down and waved at him and he waved back. I have always admired these men who ride the ranges in search of cattle and wild horses. What a hard life that must have been so many years ago. So a big salute to those who still carry on the tradition.

Rolling across the last stretches of Montana we see herds of Antelope and deer quite close to the highway. But the deer and the Antelope weren't playing. The deer were fat and their antlers were thick with velvet.

Our roads are dry, the sky is blue and the winds are still at the moment.

At Kodak, South Dakota we parked for the night and again the wind rocked us all night.

December twenty second, we are back in Wisconsin preparing for the big day with our family. We had a great time with them all and especially enjoyed watching the little ones as they opened their gifts.

After the meal the children bundled up and enjoyed sliding down their Grandpa George's hills, having the time of their lives rolling off their saucers and the snow hitting them in the face we heard the laughter as they enjoyed themselves.

Watching the children brought back our own childhood memories and made quite a conversation piece.

Two days later we were on the road again. Picking up a load in Baraboo, Wisconsin we headed for Missouri where there was snow on the road and several cars and trucks had gone into the ditch. We got to our US Mail distribution destination the next day after a good night's sleep.

We got our first drop off and headed for Coppel where we were unloaded right away and was on our way to Fort Worth B.M.S and was treated with courtesy and unloaded in good time.

Bill got his orders from the head office to go to Hockley, Texas for his pickup of salt. He delivered the salt to Louisville, Kentucky and then went into Jasper, Indiana to visit a brother and sister-in-law on New Year's Day.

We ate at Perkins restaurant and had their very delicious peanut butter pie. No one makes peanut butter pie like Perkins.

It was the first time my brother Al had ate it and they wound up buying a whole one to take home.

After spending a few hours with them, Bill headed for Owensboro, Kentucky for a pickup of paper for delivery to Woodbridge, Illinois.

We came across the beautiful new Ohio River Bridge. A new concept in design.

We haven't seen so much mud and so many muddy rivers and lakes as we have this winter.

Talk about muddy waters, we would not have wanted to encounter an off shoulder situation.

It is still raining going back across Indiana on sixty six east. Anyone could play with mud pies to their hearts content.

So much water, everything is saturated.

January, two thousand three. Leaving the Chuck Wagon Restaurant at Meade, Kansas where we had a great breakfast and good service we head for Tucumcari where we'll fuel up and roll on.

I'm reading the Truckers New Testament and as I look out the window I see the old style telephone poles that remind me of the cross that Jesus was crucified on so many years ago. The braces of the cross bar reminds me of how his arms were spread and his hands nailed to them.

Do you ever think that when Jesus gave up his life to save us from sin? Do you ever think of the terrible pain he suffered compared to what we suffer today? Our pain is not more than a point of a needle compared to his.

I'm not saying our pains are not intolerable, I have known pain of the worst kinds but I have known miracles too. Trust in the Lord and he will ease your pain.

Today we are leaving New Mexico with our load of dried milk. Rolling out across a roller coaster road on East three fifty, we can see for miles and miles ahead of us.

There are very few homes as we travel through Pueblo and Comanche territory. There are many crumbling and deserted wood and adobe homes.

Not even a train is using the silver ribbon of track that follows our road to La Junta, Colorado.

There is a small herd of cattle laying around a watering hole and we came across a couple of homes in a place called Tempas.

There are windmills scattered throughout the area to pump the water for the cattle and the few homes that are there.

Miles and miles of telephone and electric poles and fences are strung across the land.

We'd probably get excited about a car passing us if it wasn't that it seems good to be out of the rush of things.

We arrive at La Junta Milling and Elevator feed and grains and deliver our load. There is a large train terminal and several industries that give the outlying homesteaders a place to work.

Our next destination is Fort Bents Feeders, about six miles out of town to a feed lot.

The cowboys there greet us with a friendly style. A white horse stands by a rail fence waiting to do whatever is asked of him.

Hay is stacked in holding bins and along fields for feeding. It smells as a typical farm and brings back nostalgic memories of when we lived on one.

The powdered milk is mixed with the feed for the cattle.

We travel on our way to Aurora, Nebraska to pick up canned tuna. We have a layover and stay at a nice truck stop at Grand Island. Bosselman is to be congratulated on a great place.

The smoking areas are such that the non smokers don't get the drifting smoke from those who do smoke.

There is plenty of parking space and a clean yard. This is located on I eighty and two eighty one in Grand Island at exit three twelve.

In Iowa we notice how the fields are contoured on the hilly land. We assume it's to keep the water from running off too fast and causing erosion of the land.

It is a Saturday night and traffic isn't too heavy on I eighty heading for Walcott, until we get closer to Missoula where we stay at Kwik Trip with a nice restaurant.

Coming out of Iowa Eighty truck stop, we head for West Chicago for our drop.

It has been a long weekend as we have been sitting since Thursday as has other truckers. Sometimes the brokers just don't have the loads coming in.

At the forty mile marker on eighty west in Iowa, we picked up the much announced snow storm we were to get across much of the west. We had good roads until we neared Shelby, Iowa and then the storm hit with all its fury. Traffic slowed and most of the time we couldn't see more than a few feet in front of us.

The kicking up of the snow from the trucks and cars in front of us made visibility even worse, sometimes zero.

There was heavy traffic but most drivers drove sensibly. Some cars were turned around unexpectedly in the opposite way they wanted to go. Others found the ditch as did semis.

When we found a truck stop where we knew there was plenty of parking we wheeled in. We could no longer tell where the road was and other truckers followed us.

Even though the salt shakers and sand trucks with their plows were out, the snow proved too much.

This sure looked like a good old fashion Wisconsin winter to me, even though it was in Iowa.

In the morning we heard and saw what had occurred in the storm's wrath.

A semi was laid on its side and split in half and there were others on their side. One in a creek bed and another standing almost straight up where it had gone down between two bridges.

They say there is no wrath like a woman scorned. I say there is no wrath like a winter storm.

A person never gets use to driving in this kind of weather.

We head for Longmont, Colorado and park for the night and in the morning we head for Salt Lake City, Utah with our third drop.

As we roll onto two eighty seven the highway is an accident waiting to happen. It is pure packed snow and ice and there is very little signs of sand or salt. The hills are like an ice pond.

We are at twenty five and sometimes forty miles an hour. No one is passing.

With a sigh we hit the Wyoming border where the roads have been sanded and salted and are good. Maybe Colorado could learn to care for their roads from Wyoming.

It seems each time we come through Wyoming the scene changes. The ridges, hills and the snow covered mountains in the distance all present a different view.

We stop at Echo Canyon. What a beautiful sight. This was the trail of those brave Mormons who first decided to make their own Religion with Brigham Young, being their leader to help them.

What brave pioneers they were to cut out a trail for others to follow.

The men and women who followed these ancient trails and built our Interstates and bridges through these mountainous passes, have given us a bit of history we'd never see otherwise. They are to be congratulated for a job well done.

I can't imagine the work that went into putting in the railroad tracks and tunnels that the many trains run on or through.

America, America, God shed His grace on thee and Wyoming, Montana and Colorado that give us Purple Mountains of Majesty.

What a beautiful Country we have.

I often wonder how much gold is left in them thar hills?

Good morning Texas! The day has awakened before us in all its splendor and Angel Wings are spread across the sky uncovering a fire red sun to brighten up the day.

The forest of trees are spread for miles and are a great contrast to the Desert.

We see some small herds of the beautiful goats that look like the cashmere sweaters we wear.

We are in the more mountainous and populated part of Texas. Kerryville is just around the bend and we are picking up more early morning traffic.

People are on the move once again. Snowbirds, fishermen, big rigs, the four wheelers heading for work, school busses loaded with children heading for school, trains rolling along through the hills and a few planes overhead checking out things or coming in for a landing or taking off into the wild blue yonder.

Even the cattle are busy grazing and all God's creatures great and small are at work doing something.

We are rolling on through San Antonia at eight thirty in the morning and it is busy.

Four wheelers are dodging in and out of traffic.

We are up high on a bridge and my stomach drops to the floor and Bill laughs. A fender bender in the west bound lane is causing a several mile back up.

The Texas and American Flags are flying in the wind high above the streets as it should be.

We take four ten south and connect up with ten west and then ten east to Houston. We can't complain much about the Texas highways as they haven't been bad and like most states they are continuously improving them.

Bumping along into Louisiana on I-ten I could make cottage cheese out of milk in no time. What a terrible ride until we get over the bridge they have redone.

Then we hit the rib cracking bumps again.

Once again we travel across the Henderson Swamp where the bridges across are about are about thirty to forty miles long. They are worth traveling across to see.

We travel a short ways across Mississippi out of the path of my brother Harold, who likes to sweep the leaves out of the ditches as he heads down the road, as his grandson puts it.

Alabama has bridges similar to Louisiana that goes across the Gulf but not as long. The Gulf is so rough and low in spots and very muddy. We don't see any activity on it.

We spot the "U.S.S. Alabama Battleship" in dock and would like to tour it, but no time. So much to see and no spare time. Another attraction to put on our list of things to see.

As we enter Florida there is a new inspection station going up beside the Welcome Center on ten east. We are at sixty miles an hour and there is road construction ahead.

We cross Escanaba Bay and the water below us is really rough. The wind rocks us on the bridge which is a little scary.

In the evening we stay at Baldwin, eat and have a few games of cards and are in bed by nine o'clock.

We are up by six, Florida time and go to our pick up in Jacksonville, Alabama, which is only a few miles down the road. We then head for Opelika, Alabama.

There is heavy frost on everything in the morning. It got pretty cold during the night but we were able to stay warm with our heater. It was the coldest they had it since the Eighty's.

Lake Park Georgia truck stop is a good place to stop. A lot of truck drivers stop here on exit two at ten North.

The Snow Birds are moving and the RV parks are about half empty.

As we travel we see hundreds of car dealers and RV dealers waiting to sell their vehicles. It is not a good year for the sale of anything this year from the looks of it. But neither was two thousand and two.

The economy has steadily been getting worse. We see it in the trucking business, the loss of jobs, the Stock Market and the closing of factories and stores.

When are we going to wise up and keep our jobs here in the U.S.A. instead of bringing the products 'back' to America!

We are on seventy five south connecting up with eighty two west and then five twenty. We are going through the older part of Georgia. So many older homes and businesses.

We come by Plains, Georgia, home of President Jimmy Carter.

Pecans, peanuts, and cotton seems to be the main products grown here.

We stop at Opelika and watch the Super Bowl with the Raiders and Tampa Bay Buccaneers. It was a good game.

We drop our load at Wal-Mart distributing. It doesn't seem fair that they charge a Lumpers fee of eighty five dollars or more to unload the trucks, as it is their merchandise. How else would they get it if the truckers didn't deliver it to them?

The world is a thief and it is greedy.

We pick up a load of foundry forms from Calera, Alabama and head for Iowa. We run into rain, sleet and snow. The roads are icy but the crews are out sanding and spreading liquid calcium.

It doesn't take long for the roads to clear and we are on our way to Muscatine, Iowa to pick up for Heinz and deliver to Laredo, Texas on Friday.

We follow the rush hour traffic through downtown Dallas. What a sight. The huge buildings loom before us and around us. The exhaust smell is awful and we'll be glad to be out of it.

We are seeing more truck stops going to fast foods. So are we all going to get fat from them and will we sue them if we do?

As for me give me my own home cooked meals and a clean atmosphere.

Where are the inspectors who are suppose to check out restaurants. For the last four months we have seen so many dirty floors. Look under the tables and in the bathrooms that make you gag. There are waitresses with hair hanging in the faces as they serve your food.

I guess when you're hungry enough you put up with it or you move on hoping to find a clean place.

So maybe fast food is the way to go. They wear plastic gloves to handle food. Their hair is braided or tied back and the places are kept clean and the food is not dried out or cold unless you want it that way.

We are on our way again and after driving over half the night looking for a place to park our truck, we stop at Blytheville truck stop. As we came into the driveway I thought we were going to tip over. We drove into pot holes so deep 'we had no choice' and filled with water we couldn't tell how bad they were until we hit them. There were quite a few of them.

I hoped that after those few years that we had been done with trucking that they had been fixed for all those other truckers who were still out there.

Something that would be nice in these big distribution centers when a driver has to sit all day or wait for several hours to get loaded or unloaded would be a waiting area where a driver could buy a cup of coffee and a sandwich.

Some of them have a roach coach that comes around, but a lot of them don't. It can be a long day if you don't have anything with you to eat while waiting.

These drivers that travel for hundreds of miles to get these places their stuff to them on time need to be shown some appreciation.

We have been on fifty five north since last night, February first and the road is so bad that if I didn't have my seat belt on I'd be on the floor or through the windshield. Speed limit is seventy, which is good because we go over the bumps faster.

Ya! Right!

We are on north fifty seven and the bears are at the front doors and the back doors and it's really hard to stay at fifty five miles per hour when it's been sixty five to seventy and you have a clear straight road ahead and finally a decent one.

The Missouri weigh stations are open and they are checking under any truck carrying hazardous material.

We are in the slow lane today which is the right lane instead of the Hammer lane or the old name for it, The Munford Lane, The Show Off Lane or Fast Lane.

Back on the CB again, Bill got into a conversation with another driver who told him an interesting story about when he was raising sheep and all he had was a live wire fence to keep his sheep in the pasture.

The neighbor's cattle would cross over it and some of his sheep would get out and he would lose some.

He told a friend about it and asked him if he knew where he could get a good dog. The friend told him he didn't need a good dog and that he should get a Jenny - a female mule.

He told him if he got one of them he wouldn't have any more trouble losing his sheep. He told him he had one for one hundred and sixty five dollars.

So Joe told him he would be over in the morning to get it.

Joe got it and took it home and put it in with his sheep. The Mule took over the bunch of sheep like they were her babies and Joe only lost one sheep after that.

As we travel through different states, it is very strange not to see children playing outside. We see a few on four wheelers or dirt bikes or skiing.

How sad the computers, TV's and video games have taken over their minds and time.

In Wisconsin we run into snow, snow, snow. They really need it and it's about four above. BRRR!

We drop our load and have two days off and it's rush, rush, rush to get the things done we need to do.

Things just aren't that great out here on the road. Fuel goes up and down. You just don't know what you'll be paying next time you fill up.

Work is picking up a little bit for the truckers, but there are so many other workers being laid off. So many of our factory jobs are going to China, Mexico and other foreign Countries.

The slogan "Bring it back to America" is so right. But it should say "Foreign America".

What has happened to our Country, Land of the Free and plenty of jobs?

We are now prisoners of our own land of greed and joblessness, of a Government who does not care about us. But Government should remember they work for us.

Our elderly over sixty five have to work at part time at low paying jobs to make ends meet.

They should be enjoying life. They worked for their retirement years and now they work some more because the amount of Social Security our Government doles out to us is suppose to be sufficient for us to live on, even though everything keeps going up. The raises of Social Security does not keep up with the cost of food and medicines and the rest of the economy.

When I see certain people and some of the other Senators and Congress men and women standing before us and practically licking their chops thinking of the big raise they will vote themselves in the fall, we won't have a thing to say about it. Isn't it a shame that they can get whatever they want in a raise and the Senior Citizens get so little a raise.

I sometimes wonder if their parents or children are being taken care of by these high paid Senators and Congress men and women or do they have to work their way up the ladder on wages as the 'Normal Worker' does.

I think that if people want peace and equality so bad that one of these days, the Government had better get out of our way and let us have it.

As Calvin Coolidge put it, "Patriotism is easy to understand in America, it means looking out for yourself by looking out for your Country."

No matter what the American people do to show their support for the country, what we have and want, there are those in Washington who want to take it away from us and make us a dictatorship.

There are so many older men and a few women out here driving these eighteen wheelers trying to hold onto what they've worked so hard to achieve.

The young people today, trying to buy a home, raise a family and keep their bills paid are hard pressed. I feel sorry for those who work hard for these privileges just to have them taken away.

It's not fair to the parents and grandparents either to have to support them. But what can they do?

I believe in our flag flying in the wind reminding us what America was, but I cannot believe in our Government any longer. It's just taken too much away from us.

The talk of war is increasing and our men and women are being shipped to the Gulf and other strategic places.

It makes you wonder how bad it is going to be with Iraq "Saddam Hussein" and will other countries join us in the fight.

The greed, selfishness, disrespect and going against the marital way and religion has corrupted most of us.

We are having a little snow in Fremont, Indiana. But we have had quite a bit of snow where ever we go.

We are watching a herd of deer run by in a field about two hundred feet in front of us. Three get confused as the biggest share of the herd has gone on ahead and the three stand and look our way before tearing off and go into the woods.

What a sight to watch them. They are such a proud looking animal. But they can do so much damage as we all know.

Bill tells of going over Donner Pass and seven or eight deer in a row walked beside his truck. He said there was nowhere else for them to go and it was just like they were saying, "Don't push me, don't push me."

We did not realize how big an operation Family Dollar stores were until we saw their distribution center.

We are going over Black Mountain with the sunshine in our face.

We are rolling slowly through Pisgah National Forrest as we head down and then back up again. My ears keep popping and I keep yawning.

We heard again today of a few more companies folding and the truckers are complaining of no freight.

March should tell of how bad it really is.

We stop at Waynesville to fuel up at Pilot on west forty and then roll on through the Smokey Mountains. There is a little snow by the cold looking streams far below us.

There are homes built high above the Maggie Valley here in the Smokey Mountains.

The roads are winding but clear as we pass over Pigeon River and through Pigeon Forrest. Speed is fifty mile an hour and we take it slow going down.

Trash bags line some of the highways as prisoners have been out picking up trash. Today was the first time we saw a guard with a shot gun on his shoulder. It must be a scary feeling being guarded that way.

On highway sixty five just north of Columbus, we see a once in our lifetime phenomena. Snowballs of various sizes are all over the fields.

They claim it is because the wind was so strong it drew the snow from the ground and rolled it. It is quite a fantastic sight and we had to take pictures for proof. It's just so unbelievable, I'm sure it's another Ripley's Believe It or Not. There are miles of them and some were as large as hay bales.

The C.B. is busy keeping information flowing to each other on the conditions of the roads and what to expect ahead. Thank goodness for the C.B. and cell phones and the police who are out doing their jobs. And the Tow truck drivers who are out in any kind of weather doing their jobs.

America should thank the truck drivers who are out there every day in every kind of weather making sure their products get to the places that need them.

Someone is playing a harmonica and someone else is singing the words to the song on the C.B.

Much better than the foul mouths and road rage we were listening to when we had to sit because of a backup.

Most of these drivers have been out here long enough to know what to expect. But there are always butt heads out there. The backup is finally moving and the wind has gotten quite strong as we head south on sixty five.

Coming through a busy part of Nashville, we hit a busy stretch of road where large chunks of black top are hitting the under belly of the trucks and cars. Chunks are being ripped out of the road leaving good size pot holes. An accident waiting to happen.

It is raining hard and flood warnings are out. Mud slides are being reported and water is standing in various places.

We are stopped in traffic by a mud slide and trees down in the road just ahead of us. A tree has come down across a car's windshield . The older couple inside are alright but shook up.

Truck drivers and people in four wheelers are banning together to try to clear the trees from the road. Police have been called and emergency help is on its way.

There are chains and ropes and Bill has a hand saw but it is not big enough to do much good. A State trooper is out of his car and in the midst of helping to get the mess cleaned up.

Our help has arrived and in an hour one lane has been cleared and we are on our way.

There is caution as more of the hill and rocks and trees are close to coming down as water is gushing over the side.

In Alabama a little north of Troy, we find a Pioneer Village. There are several old pioneer homes and antique stores. It would be very interesting to tour them and see the history that was made in Alabama so many years ago.

I never thought history could be so fascinating. But the more we travel and the more we see, the more we realize what a fascinating world we live in.

We have a very dark and dreary day today, February seventeenth, two thousand three. But we are thankful we are not traveling in the East where they are having some terrible snow storms.

We head for Florida and it does seem good to see green grass and flowers after all the snow. It is good to be out without a lot of extra clothes on and to enjoy the warm weather.

Once again we head for North Carolina after we pick up a load of bales of cotton for our delivery.

In North Carolina there is hardly any snow to our surprise but there is considerable tree damage along the road of four twenty one from the snow storm they did have earlier.

After coming out of Cherokee National Forrest in Tennessee we have rain.

We are on west forty with Ruby Falls advertisements on bill boards. It is really an interesting and fantastic sight to see. Going below ground is rather scary but well worth it. Perhaps they have widened the passage so people don't have to pass each other side ways. It could prove to be a tight squeeze as I have put on a little weight since I was last there. I guess the years do that to a person as they get older.

Rolling over Jellico Mountain the roads are clear and good. Unlike the ones we just came over that just about bounced you out of your seat.

At Corbin we are by-passed to twenty five east because of an insulation factory blowing up. We turn off on north two twenty nine at Barborsville. Not fit for truckers to be on, too narrow, mud slides and not much of a shoulder when you meet another big rig. There is twenty one miles of this to London.

Besides the factory blow up, there is a back up because of two other four wheeler accidents. This all within a twenty five mile stretch.

Traffic is slow and drivers are getting testy.

Just heard there were twenty two people hurt and some missing in the explosion.

Well we got out of that mess and headed out on seventy five to two sixty four west and run smack dab into another back up where they are trying to pull a semi out of a deep drop off.

The only way to bring it up is up over a guard rail and onto a bridge. It has been down there since Sunday the sixteenth and this is the twentieth. They have been trying for six to eight hours to bring it up. Guess it was a piggy back and they don't have anything big enough to bring it up.

We finally get on our way and head out for New Jersey and pick up our load the next morning and run into snow at Valparaiso. It gets pretty bad and we park at Valparaiso for the night.

We had fair weather going back to Menominee, Wisconsin. The roads were clear for awhile as we headed for Allerton and Pella, Iowa.

At Hammond, Wisconsin we picked up rolls of plastic to deliver to Corona, California. It began to snow again in Kansas but it wasn't that bad.

As we neared Strong City we were delayed a short time as there was a terrible, terrible accident.

A swim coach was killed as he crossed the center lane in his hurry to get to a meeting with his correction officer.

He hit a parked semi head on at sixty five miles per hour. The semi driver wasn't hurt but awfully shook up and left with a night mare that will probably haunt him the rest of his life.

A van full of friends or relatives following the coach took to the ditch when the two front tires blew out. They were able to keep the van up right. But how sad to see someone in front of you killed that way. It's never worth the risk.

After the Coroner arrived we were allowed to leave. There was pieces of the car all over the road and the engine from the truck was laying there also.

Looks like March first of two thousand three is coming in like a Lion. But the Lamb seems to be arguing with him because we did get sunshine.

The big trucks ahead of us kick up so much road water that it's hard to keep our windshield clean. The Snow Birds are traveling east by the dozen. Must be to get home before the gas prices go up, up, up.

Rolling through Liberal, Kansas it is so gloomy we have lost our sunshine. Looks like maybe the March Lamb lost its argument.

We get some business taken care of in New Mexico and see some fellow Snowbirds and have some lunch with them. We make a trip into Polomas, Mexico. It is a bustling little town and the vendors are out in full force.

We walk across the border as it can take up to two hours or more to get out again as every vehicle is screened with a special full scanner.

It will probably be our last trip into Mexico as we got what we needed and we may not be this way again before we take a few months off for the summer while Bill has surgery.

We're hoping we can get another job in the fall as this seems to be Bill's lifeline. As the rain is to the crops so is trucking to Bill. He has had a lot of problems, but we feel they are finally getting taken care of.

So many trucks just sitting today waiting for a load.

The trucking business has taken a slow turn. Looks like there are about three to four hundred trucks sitting here.

Leaving Long Beach at about six o'clock, we are caught up in the heavy traffic. There are no bad incidents as we roll on through Anaheim, Santa Ana, Palm Springs and a few other cities.

There are yellow blossoms along the way and they just sort of brighten the day.

The Arizona dessert is the greenest we've seen it in a long time. The abundance of rain this Spring has really helped.

We wonder where the economy is going. We read in the paper this morning "The U.S.A." that there may be a shortage of gas. What else or what next will happen?

Guess we have our own little battle going on with this truck. We chugged-a-lugged a long for about fifteen miles to get to a Pilot at Phoenix to try and find out what's wrong with the thing again.

Cars and other truckers were very tolerant of our chugging along. They change the fuel filter, but it doesn't do the job. Bill talked to the head mechanic again and was sent to the Peterbilt garage just down the road. A new air filter is put on and we figure that is the end of our problem.

They take it out for a run and it seems to be alright. We hook it up to the trailer and head out. About ten miles and it is balking again. We turn around and take it back to Peterbilt.

They put it on the Dyno and they decide it is the fuel pump. They check to see if they have a pump. They had to get one from across town which took a while. It is ten o'clock and they work until midnight. Another day shot.

Rolling across Texas, Oklahoma, and Kansas we see a few oil pumps working.

The sun comes up like a ball of fire over the Kansas Prairie and it is soon covered by clouds. But the clouds move on and we have our ball of fire again.

Another week, a few more loads to haul. We are grateful we are kept busy. That is what Bill likes.

Maryland, Virginia, West Virginia, North Carolina, Pennsylvania, make for some nice trips. We are enjoying the trips even more now as it seems spring is truly on its way. So much to enjoy, rolling across America.

March seventeen, two thousand three President Bush has given Saddam Hussein an ultimatum to leave Iraq in forty eight hours or there will be war.

No one wants war but we cannot let someone as dangerous as Saddam Hussein to continue to terrorize our freedom and our country.

We wanted to fly the American Flag on the antenna of our truck and we asked at several truck stops for them but all they had were stickers or on suction cups.

We ask at some stores but they didn't carry them either.

What better way to show our support to our men and women who are serving to protect us and our country. Shouldn't this be an everyday occurrence, instead of just when we're in trouble?

And it sure seems like we're in trouble with other countries all the time.

Oh for a Miracle!

We have men and women protecting our shore lines, skies and borders every day from our enemies. I don't believe any country is totally free of terrorists or enemy action of some kind.

Our symbol of Uncle Sam seems to have disappeared and the majority of our young people's willingness to join and support or protect our country has gone by the wayside.

War was declared March nineteen, two thousand three with Iraq. It has been a week and some of our soldiers have been killed. They died bravely doing what their country asked of them.

It seems Saddam is very evasive with his many underground bunkers and tunnels. We wonder if we would be able to capture him since he seems to be every bit like Adolph Hitler.

After only six months of training at the Great Lakes Naval Base, a young friend of ours - nineteen years old - has been flown to the Gulf to take up residence on the Aircraft Carrier "Nassau".

We are wondering how long it will be before our own grandson who is twenty one years old will be sent with his ship "The U.S.S. Enterprise".

President Bush, you've taken on a tremendous task. Good Luck and God Bless.

It seems we have hauled just about everything we could, in a van or a fifty three foot trailer.

We are winding our way over a very curvaceous road - 136 east through the Sierra Madre Mountains and there are hills and valleys and small streams everywhere. We have seventy eight thousand pounds on and are in no big hurry except that we want to get off this mountain safe and sound. We have a lot of level spots so we can take a deep breath once in a while.

There are several ranches back in the hills and it must be very peaceful with only the IRS, the NFO, the Banks, the Land Management and a few I won't bother to mention. Oh well, enjoy!

We sleep at Mojave and it's a long journey across the dessert. Fifty five miles an hour in California on a wide open straight road for miles for truckers, seventy for cars and motor homes who are anything but professionals. If motor homes pulling another vehicle "without a CDL" can go this fast, why not the semis? You take a forty foot motor home or travel trailer pulling a boat or another trailer behind them and are as long as a semi, should be made to have a CDL and should have to be weighed same as a semi truck.

Did you ever look at a mountain of stones and wonder what would happen if you pulled out the right rock and they all came tumbling down? Something like playing Jenga. You wonder if the way the earth is being disturbed if that could happen.

We are curious about the Big Sky Casino in Ocoma, New Mexico, so we take our selves in there and have breakfast and do a little gambling and lose and are on our way. The machines were tight today and listening to the machines you could just about guess how they were paying out. It's a shame to watch people put hundreds of dollars into the machines and very few get anything out.

What a beautiful March day we have here in New Mexico as we travel toward our destination. On the side of a semi tractor are these words, "Three Nails, One Cross, 4 Given". What a way to remember how our Lord Jesus gave his life for us to forgive our sins. We should thank God every day and yet we keep right on sinning. But we are mortals and he keeps right on forgiving. Thank you God!

There are so many trains setting on the tracks lately that are empty, where as a few weeks ago they were heavily loaded with freight. It is rather scary as far as the economy goes.

At Pratt we pick up freezing rain but there is enough traffic to keep it from freezing on the road. We are on six eighty north going toward Omaha, Nebraska. It has warmed up some and that helps. It is quite foggy again but we will burn day light while we can.

March eighth, we unloaded our fine ground earth "Diatomaceous" which is also used in meat, hot dogs, etc, to preserve it.

Our next pick up is in North Sioux, Nebraska about two miles down the road with a load of good cookies going to Lebanon, Indiana. We are given some samples and they are great and we share them with some other truck drivers. Listening to a weather report, they are predicting rain, ice, snow and wind. Not the kind of weather anyone cares to hear when they're on the road.

The wind has picked up to forty to forty five miles per hour and we can feel it pushing at us. We have sleet and rain mixed and Bill finally stops at Peoria, Illinois for the night to get out of the wind. It rocks us all night and into the next day.

We go to Bloomington but the wind is still beating at us and we stay at the TA until Sunday morning. The yard is so full of pot holes you could almost lose a truck in them and they do not repair them. I guess they figure it's good enough for the truckers since there are a lot of truck yards like that.

Traveling on to Danville, we're in hopes of being able to watch the races, but no such luck. Bill is a race car fanatic and very seldom misses one. Dick Trickle was always his favorite though, but now he has several that he cheers on. Matt Kenseth and Kyle Bush are two of his favorites while mine is Jeff Gordon. I just wish Jeff would do better.

Still going into cold weather headed for Minnesota. Because of a break down, we wait for four hours for four pallets. The last two weeks have been hard ones. We sat most of the time and were bored out of our minds. Sure weren't making any money.

As we sat and looked at the big skyscrapers, VA buildings and other tall business places, we think of all the other ones in the big Cities. It is a grim constant sad reminder of the Twin Towers terrorist attack and it will forever be in our thoughts. It seems the good ole USA has fallen into a greedy trap and nobody really isn't doing anything to make it right again. It just seems to get worse. God forbid we have another terrorist attack which I think it's possible.

Back at St. Paul at Roc Ten, we pick up a load of printed paper which we will deliver to Methuen, Massachusetts. It is good to see there are places like this to recycle the used paper products instead of burning it and polluting the air.

The sun is warm and we roll our windows down and watch the snow and ice melt and run into the drains. It makes you feel like wanting to be home, looking forward to Spring and Summer.

A lot of the fun has been taken out of driving a big rig. The fifty five mile speed limit, the date on the Log book and not being able to fuel where you want to when you need to and almost no toll roads even when it's a shorter route. The sitting, waiting to be loaded or unloaded is the hardest besides the unholy prices charged at a truck stop for a meal.

They think the truckers make big bucks and can afford it. Wrong! Those truckers are trying to buy a house, pay for a truck of their own, pay child support, taxes, feed, clothe and educate a family and pay high price insurance. When you think of what they make in gross - think of what they have left over after Uncle Sam gets his share.

You're dammed if you do and dammed if you don't. But it seems somewhere, somehow the truckers should be given a break.

I ride with my husband most of the time and I know there are other wives who do also and we know what they have to put up with day after day. It's a shame that some trucking companies still get away with paying twenty eight cents a mile. Would they work for that? I think not. How about at least forty cents.

We back up to our trailer to hook up and darned if the person who had it before us didn't drop it too short so we can't get under it or raise it. So now we wait for a yard man to come and lift it. Shifts are changing so here we sit again, waiting. "Wasted time and Wasted Days". What a bummer.

We roll up over the Snowshoes which aren't really all that steep but the pull is slow. One of our favorite eating places is at the foot of the Snowshoes at Lamar because the food is hot, fast and the service is friendly and the whole place sparkles.

Just a few are fast, friendly service, good food, decent prices, clean showers and rest rooms, a lounge, laundry and a place to park that isn't full of pot holes.

Rolling out of Lamar toward Williamsport, it is so foggy we can't see but a shadow of a vehicle ahead of us. The sun is coming out hot and bright to burn it off.

There is no snow anywhere and the last we saw was in Minnesota and Wisconsin. At the weigh stations they are checking log books and permits. A few of us escape it this time as they wave us on.

We stop at Scanton to eat, shower, and fuel. We roll east on eighty four over the Poconos where there are several junk yards in the hills. Need parts? Go for it.

Coming down off the Poconos we come into Connecticut and head for Massachusetts, where we find our drop destination and spend the night and then go to Littleton for our pickups. This will give us four drops. One in Richmond, Virginia, Durham, North Carolina, Charlotte, North Carolina, and Norcross, Georgia. So we will put on some miles again.

Having taken care of our business there we stop near Damascus, Maryland at a truck stop where we will meet with a sister and brother-in-law and visit for a couple of hours. They do not live far from the truck stop but we decide not to go to their place as we need to get an early start in the morning. I have not seen her in seven years. She is quite a talker so the conversation is pretty much one sided.

Our little dog has to go potty and there is no place to take her yet. Even dogs can only hold it for so long and she did. She is really a great dog.

We move on to West Virginia and first drop. It has been foggy and raining with some sleet. No complaints on the rain, they need it so bad in the East and of course other places as well.

We head for North Carolina again. The trees are in blossom showing their beautiful colors of pink and white. The Daffodils so pretty in their dress of yellow. We come by the huge Phillip Morris Headquarters. From the looks of the cars in the parking lot, they employ a lot of people.

Coming into Durham, North Carolina we make our second drop and head for Charlotte with our third. It's a tight squeeze to get to the dock but with a lot of maneuvering Bill gets the trailer in its proper place and is unloaded right away.

Some of the places Bill has to go to are so messy it's a wonder any one can get a truck into the dock, let alone the yard. We really appreciate the companies that make room for the trucks to get in and out of.

We're rolling again to North Carolina to our drop and then on to Moriesville for a pick up. The red slippery clay extends across South Carolina, North Carolina and Georgia. Because of the rain we're very careful not to get into any of it.

We are climbing Black Mountain and the rock walls are a black color with the leafless trees shrouded in fog. It's a scary ride across but there is plenty of traffic and a wide load ahead of us which would make it hard to pass if anyone wanted to.

The Smokies are a long pull and water gushes down the rocks in several places. There is white water rafting in the river far below and it looks rough and high.

We rumble across Tennessee and Kentucky and it's clouding up again. There is a lot of rock that has fallen by the wayside. There are still reminders of the ole Kentucky homes as there are reminders of the ole plantation Negro homes in South Carolina. There is a lot of history for everyone out here.

We are in some of the flooded area of Kentucky as we head out on eighty five, forty, eighty one and seventy five to sixty four to sixty five and we find ourselves going through what is like a rock tunnel.

It is the twenty first of March. I wonder what March will go out like.

In Indiana on north sixty five, we cross the Ohio River and see it is muddy and swollen. We have a little snow, hardly worth mentioning and we go from fifty degrees to twenty seven degrees and colder in the night. But we are cozy in our tractor bunk and snuggle together.

Our tractor is serviced at the company's yard. Full service including four new tires, wash job, new windshield, oil change etc. Since October twenty six, two thousand one, we have put on over sixty two thousand miles.

We know there are truckers out rolling these highways and byways who, like Bill, has put on a million miles since first starting to drive, which was in the early sixties.

Taking some time away from driving and trying something else for awhile never worked for Bill. It was never long before he was right back at it again.

It wasn't that he always enjoyed it, but he was trying to give his family a decent life. He knew it was a steady job and he did make money. It takes a very dedicated woman to be a truck driver's wife and to help keep the family together and things running smooth while he is gone. Of course that works both ways and it depends on how strong the love is between them.

Whenever Bill has taken time off from the truck, I tell him I am going to have the doctor take all the old blood out of him that has all these little microscopic semis in it and give him a transfusion of new blood. I guess when you have been driving for so many years it's hard to give it up. It must be like a smoker and nicotine.

Gosh, here we go in Ohio again and the cops are thicker than fleas on a dog.

We come into New Jersey on eighty west. I love this interstate because it is so nicely marked with white broken lines and reflectors which makes it so easy to see each lane and makes it easier for passing when there is so much traffic. This would be ideal on the black top highways that are miserable to see when it is raining out at night.

Construction, construction, construction and tolls. Where ever we go, whatever state, they're trying hard to build and repair, but with all the building of new bridges and roads, repair work is falling badly behind.

We don't see too much of Delaware as we pass through a corner of it into Maryland where we stop at Petro for brunch and an hour's nap.

Following ninety five south we roll along with the ribbon of tail lights that are brightening up the highway. Traffic is heavy but the roads and weather are good.

We are climbing the Cumberlands on sixty eight west and what a view. Although it is dark, the lights from the valley far below sparkle in the night like a thousand stars.

Near Haystack Mountain and Daus Mountain, I look over the side of the bridge and the roof tops of the big old three story houses come just above the bridges. I feel as though I could step out onto them.

We cross the Continental Divide at twenty six hundred feet and crawl down with our heavy load and back up again. It's a long way across.

Wide loads and oversize loads are ahead of us with flashers going and several escorts warning the other traffic of the danger.

We catch seventy nine north and the large trucks are parked along the shoulders, too tired to go further and the truck stops are full.

It is raining on this early spring morning of March twenty six here in Pennsylvania. It's a good whoopee-do day and snooze day. We have a good breakfast at TA at Dallas Pike.

The long winding streams snake their way along the highways and through the woods running over rocks and fallen logs.

Where's my fishing pole?

We go through the Wheeling, West Virginia tunnel into Ohio. It is very hazy and everyone is running with lights and wipers on and at a slower pace.

The trees are ice covered for a ways and there are big rigs heading south with snow on their roofs. We are forty miles out of Columbus, Ohio where they have snow, ice and rain. But so far the roads are fair. Indiana has more of the same as does Illinois.

We pull into a truck stop for the night and I guess they don't believe in plowing out the yard. There aren't many trucks in yet and it's a perfect time to clean out the yard.

In the morning, there are signs of drivers having thrown out their garbage out in the yard. There are garbage containers for that but some just don't give a damn. It's too bad because it gives the rest of us a bad reputation.

Going through the Illinois toll, one truck driver is using such filthy language no one can say anything unless he comes back with the F- word. The men aren't the only ones who talk this way, the women have gotten just as bad and it is really sad because what must their children think.

We both wish we were a cop about this time and be close enough to grab them by the collar and drag them out of the truck and bounce them on their head, or better yet take a plunger and plunge those dirty words back down their throats. These people are a disgrace to our society.

It is Good Friday and we are headed home for a couple of days.

There is something to like about every state we've been in. It isn't the tall sky scrapers, though they are interesting, and the lights of the city at night so much as it is the beauty of the land. The plowed fields, green pastures, the trees that are leafing out and the flowers that are blooming in their many colors and the many animals that are coming out to enjoy life.

I wonder if animals get cabin fever.

An abandoned house stands off in the distance. It's walls crumbling and the roof fallen in. A door and a couple of windows are still intact. A haven for birds and small wild animals.

Using our imagination as we ponder the different shapes of rocks, we see Elephant foot tracks and Gorillas with their large heads resting among other ones. We imagine a formation of a man standing and guarding his family. We can imagine that it has taken over a thousand years for these transformations to have taken place.

I imagine how it was when the Indians roamed these lands and taught the white people to grow crops and do many other things. While it was a hard life, I'm sure anyone can see how over the years we gained so much knowledge from them.

Each generation passing new knowledge on. Progress, some bad, some good. It goes on because I'm of the old school and I can feel that the world is moving too fast.

Perhaps if we'd all worship our God and keep our faith in him as the Indians and our forefathers did many generations ago, we would be a much better world. What happened to our beliefs?

Have we not learned anything of what happened so many generations ago when the world of the Indians was so drastically changed? Now we are coming into the same situation by letting our country be taken over by foreigners and by sending our young men into wars we cannot win.

The one thing they cannot take away from us is our belief in God. People try but I hope to God we never let them.

I hope America wakes up soon as I would not like to think what our grandchildren and great grandchildren would have to face and try to straighten out. What a mess we are in already.

Thank goodness there are other things to keep our minds occupied with and get it off these awful things that are happening to our nation, even if it isn't for long.

Perry, Florida. The place time forgot. They built it, the people live there and time more or less stood still. It's like they have all that they need right there. It seems they are happy with what they have and don't need the higher taxes or try to keep up with the Jones's. I think maybe that is something that is wrong with the rest of America today. We over live our resources and even the Jones's go down the tubes.

It doesn't look like they are asking for a lot, just enough to be comfortable. And it looks like they have that. They have family, friends, good neighbors, a roof over their heads, a job to take care of their needs, a school and a church to worship in on Sunday. What more could a person want?

We talk and think progress and where has it got us? When the big businesses from larger cities came to the town where I lived for many years with their big ideas, it wasn't long before they took over and everything was changed.

We lost a lot of our landmarks, our trees, our tourist business, our downtown Friday night visits and the closeness of neighbors. Now it seems no one has time to get to know their neighbors. We could trust one another then.

Bah Humbug! I for one would like "my" world back.

One of my biggest complaints when going down the highway is seeing some one's dead pet lying there and left to be mangled by oncoming traffic. If you have a pet, protect it with a fence or leash. If you grow tired of it or don't have time for it any more, for the love of the Pet give it to the Humane Society.

As you can see, I'm writing this as we go down the highway and as we see these interesting aspects of life that we may never see again, we would like to share them with others and be able to look back on our many travels and revisit these scenes again in our minds. We hope there will be others as interested in our travels as we are and perhaps someday will see some of these sights.

Morton Salt - what a place. Now I know where Morton salt comes from. There are large sprawling brick buildings with cat walks from building to building in the upper stories. Pipes running from the refinery to a salt pit where the salt is as white as new fallen snow. Yellow forklifts unload our merchandise with care and store it in a dry area.

The big eighteen wheelers pull in and out getting loaded or unloaded. Security is strict and OSHA makes their visits keeping an eye on things.

The tight backing to the green canopied docks with a fifty three foot trailer calls for an experienced professional truck driver. We think the docks were meant for a forty eight footer since these docks were built when there were only straight backs.

Large feeder pens for cattle can be seen and some of the bigger ones are located around Liberal, Kansas and Winnemucca in Nevada.

Oklahoma and Indiana also have large Dairy farms. It is interesting to see the hundreds of cattle lined up by the feeders and how clean the yards are kept. We see men in the yards with large tractors with buckets on them cleaning up what the cattle leave behind. There are others who are taking feed out to the troughs for the cattle. Hay is piled high in covered buildings for year round feedings.

The feeder pens where the cattle are kept that are soon going to market would pose a problem to be kept clean. But the cattle are not there that long when you can see large trucks being loaded.

At night we try not to park near them as the smell is horrendous and you can hear the cattle stomping and bawling all night.

A story is told of a group of men standing near a cattle truck discussing the price of them and as they talked, one of the truckers moved like lighting. To his vast surprise one of the animals decided to let loose and as it did it squirted out of one of the holes and all over the fast moving trucker.

"Aw Shit!" He yelled.

"You got that right." Replied another and they had a good laugh over it.

A sign along the highway on east sixty nine near Muskego, Oklahoma read "Lotawatah". Up the road a ways we came upon a large body of water.

I laughed, looking over at Bill and said, "Lot-a-watah".

He said "What!"

I replied, "That's a Lot-a-watah."

He got the pun. I think that will be one of my favorite words.

Listening to Paul Harvey on the radio, he told about some business men passing through Nacogdoches. One of the men tried to figure out how to pronounce the name. As they neared a Dairy Queen, they stopped and asked the young man behind the counter how to pronounce the name of the place. The young man looked at them and said very slowly, "Dairy Queen."

I always enjoyed listening to Mr. Harvey. Especially when he would tell "the rest of the Story". Another great News caster was Gabriel Heater. I always thought he should run for President of the United States.

We are going through Gallup, New Mexico. What beautiful scenery with smooth rock walls so high it looks like they meet the sky. The falling of stones has carved large caves where a person could stand and observe what's around you.

The Arizona Welcome Center and the Yellow Horse Tourist attraction is located there.

The snow on the mountains give added beauty to the red coloring of the rocks.

This is Indian Territory and you can buy beautiful pottery and other Indian artifacts. Beautiful blankets, belts and turquoise jewelry and many other items.

We are leaving Gallup and are six thousand feet up heading for Flagstaff. It is January sixteen and the weather looks good. The streams are badly dried up and they could use some rain or snow. I'm sure each Eighteen Wheeler that goes over Flagstaff prays for good roads and good weather. It can get pretty treacherous otherwise.

We have left the residential communities behind and are traveling over a very bumpy highway forty going west through barren land.

We make up our own scenes such as clouds in the shape of a Capital Dome or Angel Wings or two people kissing or feathery horses prancing about.

In the distance we see a hill with shrubs dotting the top of it but it looks more like Buffalo marching down it in single file. Try using your imagination when you're out side and look upward to see what you can see.

The far plateaus look like a place you'd like to have a picnic on. The landscapes present varied forms of entertainment for the sight seers, tourists, rock hounds and the mind.

It's easily imagined how the Indians lived out here, but hard to realize they made a living from that land and could still enjoy what they had. Imagine what they would have given to be able to go to a store and trade for what they needed.

On top of Flagstaff we hit sleet and snow, but only for a short time. We leave that behind in a hurry.

We hit Phoenix and get a glimpse of it bathed in bright lights as we travel to our destination for our eight o'clock drop.

Our Schnauzer sleeps on the driver's seat at night and during the day she thinks she owns it. She hasn't learned to drive yet, so she does have to share it and so she sleeps on the floor or shares my seat so she can look out the window.

She's gotten awfully spoiled in the truck though. She expects us to bring her a treat every time we stop to eat. Her usual treat from the truck stop is chicken. After wards she has to have a drink and the water sits on the floor next to her.

She won't turn around enough to get her drink and she looks at us with her big brown eyes and woofs until one of us gives it to her. Is that old age that makes us wait on one another? She is going on twelve years and she's worth spoiling.

We dropped our load of paper products and have a twenty four hour layover. It's a warm sixty three degrees, so we don't mind.

We pull into the Flying J truck stop in Phoenix, but it is already full of the big trucks and there is no place to park. Other truckers are also on lay over waiting to drop their loads or for a pick up.

Some have just come in for a shower, something to eat or to fuel up. We like the idea there were no cars to worry about. Across the road is Danny's Big Rig Parking and we go there. We pay so much to park, depending on how long we'll be there. It is well worth it.

They have cart shuttle service, truck washing and repair and a parts store. We were impressed with their large lounges for the drivers, a place to relax or watch TV and everything is immaculate. It's a no nonsense place and you do not throw your garbage out on the ground or pee in the yard or you get booted out.

There is no restaurant so we had to walk back to the flying J. As we did we noticed the water falls at Danny's and the hard smooth lot where the trucks could be shined up.

We were impressed with the scenery between the two trucks. The restaurant was quite packed. It was quite large and the waitresses very neat and friendly and we received very good service.

It was one truck stop we didn't get tired of waiting for our waitress or food. Everything was good and we had their Buffet.

Except for a very few, truck stops across America used to be a great place to stop. But now food prices are higher and bath rooms and showers are in pretty bad shape. Chicken on most buffets is so breaded and crisp and only half done, it sure doesn't look eatable and you wonder where the chicken is. The desserts are left uncovered and dry out.

We really did enjoy our meal at the Flying J and browsing through the store.

We go back to Danny's Big Rig and shower and then head for our truck. We play a few games of cards and go to bed early so we can be on time for our pick up of Pepsi products.

Trucks are coming and going, security is tight and the yard is clean and all trucks are checked by security. After we're checked out, seal put on and papers signed, we head for Petro Truck Stop to eat. The food would have been good if it hadn't been cold.

Another beef about public bath rooms. If you're going to put a door on a toilet stall, why not make it so you have some privacy instead of such big cracks in them any one can look in on you. And why have stalls where the sinks and mirrors are right in front of them so people can look in on you. I like my personal business to be my own.

I'm really impressed with some of the new sinks at some of the waysides. You put your hands under the faucet to start the water that is mixed with soap to wash the hands. Then clear water rinses your hands and when done, a blower comes on to dry them. You don't have to touch a thing. Now that's progress I like.

January eighteen, we're now crossing the Arizona desert again going east. Cactuses are prevalent, but not yet in bloom. There is advertisement of Rex Allan's Museum at Wilcox and Texas Canyon which we are passing through.

RV parks are plentiful throughout Arizona. Even boon docking is allowed and fun if you don't mind roughing it.

There are a lot of campers on the road heading East. This is part of what makes trucking so interesting. Seeing so much of what goes on out here on the highways and how other communities are developed and how other people live.

Groves and groves of pecan trees and walnuts are scattered throughout the areas.

The mountain ranges are all around us here in New Mexico. Cattle can be seen grazing in the distance and water is pumped into large tanks for them as the land is so alkaline.

Long trains rumble across the desert hauling products that will be shipped in the box cars consigned to be shipped that way.

Dust Devils can be seen swirling across the desert. Some get quite large and can do a lot of damage if you get caught in one.

Living in Deming, New Mexico one fall I was cleaning the camper and had the door to it open and I didn't see one coming toward us and needless to say the camper and I got a dirt bath. I had to clean the camper all over again.

A small herd of Antelope can be seen feeding off the Buffalo grass or young tumble weed plants. They are a trim, sleek beautiful animal.

Once again we visit some friends in Deming, play cards - which Mary Jane won - and have a piece of her delicious chocolate cake. Her husband, Wayne, paints and has some beautiful pictures he has done.

Pizza was on order for the next day at the Pizza hut. We had a great time but all too soon it ended and we were on our way to San Antonio to be ready to drop our load on Monday.

Deming is a busy little town and they are constantly trying to improve. It is an old but interesting place and has many small RV parks where it is easy to meet and get to know each other. If you're a rock hound, it is a great place to go.

Heading for O'Dessa, there are herds of deer to my left and goats and sheep on either side of the highway. Some herds of goats that are a beautiful white and it looks like they are covered with a smooth brushed angora blanket.

It's January twenty first and fifty degrees. Makes you feel like stopping for a picnic. But duty calls.

We have stopped to fill our cups with morning coffee and get a couple of sweet rolls to eat on the go.

It's inventory time once again and the big trucks find themselves waiting for a load.

The road crews who cut through the mountains made traveling through the walls of limestone a nice view. I wonder how long those walls will stand. We see new chunks fall daily from the vibrations of the traffic and the weather doing its part.

Closer to Odessa we spot the tall white electric generators. They remind me of Ballerinas dancing in the wind.

This is oil country! There are large oil fields dotted with many oil pumps that are working. The sign says Chevron USA. I would say there is oil in that ground. Except for the oil fields there is nothing on three twenty nine to Crane and Odessa.

We finally stop to eat at Rip Griffith at Big Springs and then drive for a few more hours since eating and being able to relax a little, we're both wide awake.

It is raining but the truckers are moving out. They are something like the Mail Carriers. Neither rain, nor snow, nor sleet nor hail can keep them from delivering their products. It can slow them down but not stop them.

Remember, without trucks America stops.

We are heading East on eight twenty toward Berne, Indiana. The DOT are pretty thick and are checking trucks. We take thirty five west and turn on three eighty east through Denton, Texas.

We encountered an over sized load of an eighty foot by sixteen foot trailer. The oversize loads are fairly common on the highways. Most often the over size or wide loads have an escort.

We stop in Durant to mail an overnight UPS letter. Mailing on the road can be a problem but for ordinary mailing and UPS most truck stops will accommodate us.

Back in the wide open spaces, we miss a fresh dead skunk. It stinks to high Heaven for quite a ways. Bill says that if you hit one, a gallon of bleach poured over the tires will get rid of the smell. I guess he has had a run in with them before.

So watch out for those wood kitties or as we call them the Avon lady.

Whoops! Alligator on the road and some trucker has lost a tire. They can really make a mess when they blow and you don't want to run over any of it.

What a large beautiful lake the Eufaula is. I saw no RV parks nearby but it looked like public access. We wonder what fish are biting?

The south Canadian River looks rough and muddy today but perhaps there is good fishing.

We see signs posted along several highways that read "God Bless America". But a big sign we saw asks "how can God bless America when we kicked him out of our schools!" Why do we let a few people tell us how we can use our Religion?

The big rigs are rolling tonight and it is a sight. We have a convoy! Another trucker asks what our twenty is, and Bill says bring it on back.

In answer, the trucker says, "Red Rose running at my front door. Come on."

"Affirmative!" Replies Bill. "Topped one mountain climb and began on the downhill slide."

"Back atcha. That's a ten four. Settled in seat and shifted gears."

These truckers have their own kind of speed but it's always a pleasure to travel with them and when they shove-er down, we back down and let them fly.

Trucking is a lonely life and they pay a high price for it sometimes. And contrary to what people think, it is not an easy life. Sometimes families travel together for a few days, but there is not much room to be comfortable for long.

One driver told of receiving a divorce as a Christmas present. He was only forty five. He figured she liked money more than him and he just wasn't making enough for her.

Another young man's wife just up and left him - after she cleaned out his bank account.

An older gentleman said he had two more years to go and he would have forty years in and then he was going to enjoy his children and great grand children. He spoke so proudly of them all.

That's a big ten four, and we sincerely hope he can. It isn't very often we meet the same trucker twice. We very seldom see any one from the same company out here that we drive for. Bill would rather drive for someone else than own his own rig.

He owned his own tractor once but found out that he only inherited someone else's problems.

Indianapolis, Fort Wayne are two very busy Metropolis. So many fender benders today. Seems like the four wheelers are in a hurry to get somewhere but some end up nowhere. In three months time we have seen more accidents where so many young people were killed, sometimes whole families.

What a shame it is for some of us to learn to slow down and use caution. Is anything so important that it means we can risk some one's life? It reminds me of the song "I Heard the crash on the Highway, But I didn't hear nobody pray".

It's amazing, but a very few of these accidents involve a big truck because of the professionalism that the truck drivers show. And the little car seems to think they can get by the big truck when they come off a ramp instead of yielding to them like the signs say.

To hear some of them talk, some of the immature drivers would just as soon run over a four wheeler if they got in their way. These and the garbage mouths need to be taken off the road. But who is going to do it?

At Fort Wayne we pick up a load of baled foam rubber pieces going to Chicago.

I walk the dog and she walks me. We collect our papers and bill of lading and are on our way again toward West Chicago.

We pull in to a TA about four AM and have a very late breakfast and we are in bed by seven thirty.

We are up at three thirty AM to get coffee and head for our drop. We are early so as to miss most of Chicago's early morning traffic. We drop our load at West Chicago and head for Beloit for a pick up.

We call this Big Rig our motor home. We live in it twenty four hours a day and for now it suits us and has for about seven years, off and on, mostly on. We have just about everything we need in it.

Our bunk is three quarters wide and big enough for the two of us. We carry extra sheet sets and blankets. We have an extra bunk but we don't use it. A lot of drivers use it for storage or when they take some of the family along.

Our two closets hold our four sets of clothes and extra food. Our electric cooler holds a loaf of bread, butter, cold meat, cheese, bottled water and Mountain Dew. We always try to keep at least two or three gallons of water on hand. Wet ones are a big help for washing up between showers.

We have writing material, playing cards, which is a big pass time for us when we have to sit. We also carry other necessities like a whisk broom and dust pan and of course a porta potty and dog food.

Flash lights, a camera or two and plastic wear are tucked away where we can get at them.

Bill's atlas, mileage book, truck stop book and log books are always within reach.

While there isn't too much I can do while were moving down the highway over bumpy roads - and there are a lot of them - I read a lot. A lot of what I have read and continue to read I am now seeing what the real places are like and what the author is talking about in her or his book.

I also do Word Search and embroidery to keep myself busy. If we get on a quiet road, Bill and I can then talk to each other. It is aggravating when we try to talk to one another and the truck is so noisy we have to practically yell at each other. I also sleep when I get bored. Then I know it's time for me to take a week off from the truck.

Bill has the CB so he can talk to the other drivers and that helps him a lot. They exchange a lot of information and a lot of stories.

While Bill is out on the docks making sure his products are being handled right, I wash windows and mirrors and clean the floor and wipe off the instrument panel and dash and walk the dog.

After the September Eleventh thing, Nine-o'one-o'one we see more American Flags flying high in the air and on trucks and cars than ever before. They are a sight to behold as we travel across America and see the Red, White and Blue unfurl in the wind.

The billboards that show every kind of appreciation to our country and those who stand united with us are many. Shouldn't we always stand up and fight for what is ours and not let anyone take it away from us? What are our young men and women fighting for if we don't stand together now and do our share.

That Grand Old Flag has flown over our land for centuries and through many wars.

To show how our children have been neglected in the education of the Flag, Bill and I were at a race and we were all asked to stand for the singing of the National Anthem.

A young man of about seventeen or eighteen laughingly stood and turned to a buddy and asked what he was suppose to do? WE were disgusted that he did not know what our Flag meant to our Country.

It would be a great idea to bring back the draft and have them learn. Our young men and women are so badly in need of discipline and respect, it's tragic to see how they are turning out without parents to guide them. Too many are bringing themselves up and have no guide lines.

Let the Flag fly high and God Bless America and our Men and Women who are protecting our country from terrorists and people like Osama Bin Laudin and Sadam Hussein.

Loaded with cardboard at Beloit, we head for Janesville to get our first meal of the day. It is now twelve noon. Yes we're hungry. Our belly button is scraping against our back bone. Ouch! We always get good service and food here.

Got to remember to put a coat on as we're in a colder climate, Wisconsin. We drop our load in Viroqua and head for the company yard to pick up new orders for our next trip.

We're up at five and get our daily amenities out of the way and head for Roseville, Minnesota.

They call the web of intersecting bridges and roads, the mix master or Spaghetti Bowl.

Traffic runs smoothly and we are at our destination early. We don't have to wait long to get loaded. Other truckers are pulling in to take their turn.

Speaking of the Mix Master or Spaghetti Bowl, it is such a conglomerate of roads and bridges, it reminds you of the hundreds that are being built right now in New York, Oregon, Chicago, Texas and just about anywhere you go. It is very interesting to watch them build them.

Again the truckers are on their CB'S warning others that a west bound bear is setting on the shoulder, so watch out.

Someone comes back and tells the other trucker to leave them alone as they have to have their doughnuts and coffee too.

Some Mexicans are carrying on a conversation which goes on for quite awhile and one of the truckers yells out that he can speak Mexican too and to prove it he says 'Taco, Dorito, and enchilada'.

Then you get these jerks that have toys in their trucks with a recording device, that think it's funny when you tell them to get off the air because of their dirty language and they play the recording over and over. But we figure they don't have any brains anyway.

What a day it would be to be able to listen to the CB and not hear someone tearing into another one.

Bill told me how once he got so tired and taught himself a tremendous lesson. Driving down the highway he saw a car ahead of him and suddenly it split in-two. One half to his left, the other to his right and then as he watched, it slowly came together again, but only to split a few more times. He always knew the whole car was in front of him but his mind was playing tricks on him because he was so tired.

There was no place he could pull off until he got off the free- way. There were no shoulders wide enough and if there had been they aren't suppose to sleep on the shoulder of the road.

If you do get caught at it, you can get a hefty fine, asked for the log book and hassled in other ways. So they can't sleep any ways no matter how tired they are. Most drivers won't let themselves get in this predicament and this was an unusual one and a valuable lesson learned.

Usually a driver will take a break after sitting and driving for four or five hours. When you're young you think you can go forever, but you do learn differently.

A trucker told of another driver who had fallen asleep and was killed. As he went to meet ST. Peter, he saw this beautiful truck stop. It had a magnificent swimming pool, restaurant, anything a driver could desire.

As he drove through the area he noticed all the beautiful trucks parked there.

When he met St. Peter he asked why there were no drivers for the trucks. ST. Peter looked at him and answered, we don't have any dispatchers here.

Some of the truckers names used for different trucks or other things are like Thermos Bottle for a tankard. Piggy Back for two trailers being hauled together. Weigh Station is called a chicken coop. Bob-tail-dropped trailer and park tractor. DOT in the Pickle patch - Inspector in rest area.

Got our last drop off and am sitting and waiting to move on.

"Nine o'clock, call me back in an hour."

"Ten o'clock, head out on seventy west, call me back in an hour and a half."

"Have three loads but haven't decided which one to give you." Replies our dispatcher.

We crossed over into Alligator Alley, watching for alligators to poke their noses above water or to lay on the banks of the channels.

We have no air conditioning and it is a scorcher and humid. Whew! I assume the water in the channels is warm and there is no movement of the water. It would be interesting to take a tour of the Everglades on a wind machine.

Our highway is as straight as an arrow. Not much to see at all.

Thursday, the temperature is around ninety four degrees or higher. We finally had our first turn of the straight as an arrow road at mile marker seventy four.

A little further on there are two Alligators laying in the sand near the edge of the water in the Cypress Garden Reserve.

They have a load for us out of Ocala, Florida but can't pick it up until Saturday morning. Someone goofed and didn't get a load number for us and we could have picked the load up at nine o'clock. But it is now ten o'clock and just got the bill of laden number and still have about fifty to sixty miles to go.

We are dead heading more than four hundred miles and don't get paid for it. But that's part of trucking. That has been the way of it for the last three trips. It really hasn't been worth it, but happy to say we'll be cleaning out our truck when we get back to the yard and quit.

We did get a motel at Ocala after suffering for two days and nights in the truck. What a comfort it was at the Days Inn. We're hoping the owner of the truck will pick up the tab. We would have headed for home but would have had to wait until we got to Georgia to fill up to have enough fuel to take us home.

It is Monday, June twelfth. After having the summer off we are back on the road again with another company.

Guess we should not have got out of bed this morning. According to Murphy's law, anything that could go wrong did. A phone call from the trucking company told us we should be loaded by ten and we could start our trip to Florida with our load of paper.

Going to the yard, thirty miles from Stevens Point, Wisconsin we discover the trailer still sits in the yard somewhere. At the mill we're told they can't find the trailer because someone else pulled it there.

So we are sent to another yard, it might be there they said. It wasn't. So Bill goes back to the first mill warehouse and drives around looking for our trailer. It is nowhere in sight.

Finally, really frustrated, we go back to the company yard. The wrong pick up number is on the bill of laden. We are told we should be loaded by one o'clock. Bill has three hours to kill. Aargh!

We go to some friends and play cards trying to relax. At one o'clock we go back to the mill to get our trailer and leave for Florida.

Needles to say, they haven't been able to find the trailer. Anger sets in and then we're told it was parked with a bunch of other empty trailers in the drop yard. We feel it was deliberately done.

Ready to give up the trip entirely, we find the trailer in back of a bunch of others. If Bill could have found the jerk that did it, thinking it was funny, he may have had a trip to pay for because he cost us time and money.

We sit for another hour waiting to get loaded. Once loaded we go to the weigh scale and we're three thousand, seven hundred pounds over on the trailer axles. Bill has them redistribute the weight. He weighs again and he is still thirty two hundred pounds over. They try again, we weigh again. We're still over. Disgusted, Bill moves the axles three holes and he is finally alright.

Bill leaves the mill yard and is no sooner down the road and something snaps. He has no speedometer readings. Again disgusted, he takes it back to the company yard. It's now eleven AM. Bill says to hell with it and we go to bed.

In the morning he's told to take the truck to Madison to Freight Liner and get it fixed.

It's ten thirty in the morning and Bill is waiting his turn in the garage.

Maybe he'll get to Florida yet. He has four drops. It's three on Thursday morning and nobody seems to care when we leave, but we'd better be in Jacksonville on Thursday morning. Maybe we will and maybe we won't.

It's Fathers Day, Sunday and we had plans. Guess you don't make plans when you drive over the road.

It's gotten so the truck driver is a lowly pee-on and nobody gives a damn about them. Yet they're the ones that keep America running.

It is eleven forty and the truck is in the freight liner shop. It doesn't take the mechanic long to fix the speedometer. Bill is finally on his way again, hopefully without any more problems.

They say everything happens for a reason. We'll see.

Hurricane Alberto was suppose to blow into Florida on Monday, and hopefully by Wednesday it will be over the worst of it.

Going over Mont Eagle we have a six degree downgrade. We're at twenty five miles per hour while other eighteen wheelers are flying by us. But that is probably because they are empty.

There are ramps for run-a-way trucks and so far Bill hasn't had to use them. We have a load of paper with a weight of about seventy thousand, eight hundred pounds. Going down the mountain Bill keeps a steady three pounds of pressure on the brakes. He tells me a person should not feather them because they will get hot in a hurry.

It's a beautiful view as we go down off of Mont Eagle. From Illinois we notice a lot of old familiar names gone from some of the trucks and new ones on them. The Logistics slogan has become quite popular.

Some of the trucks out on the road are Dean Foods, Sparhawk, Wayne, Lawrence, Wal-Mart, JB hunt, Yellow, Schneider, Landstar, Missela Valley, Moodie, H.O.W, Nancy Bare, Tomah Transit, Kohel and many, many more. They come and they go.

La Belle, Florida, a cozy town. Wished we had more time to see more of it. The large trees are so gnarled and moss and old vines grow on the trunks and branches and gives them a weird and scary look.

The brush and old Palm trees along E eighty seem to shut out the traffic world until we move further away from the town. We picked up a load of water melons a few miles out of La Belle. What an experience. Even getting lost.

At Clewiston we stopped at the truck stop for breakfast. Stayed overnight at the Water melon patch until they loaded us at about ten o'clock in the morning.

They gave us a sample and two to take with us. Those were some very delicious water melons.

Heading toward seventy five a baby alligator had somehow found his way to the road and gotten killed.

On highway seventy five another one had been killed. There are deep channels all along the roads. Bill would have liked to picked it up to take back to a friend of ours. But he knew it was illegal to do so.

We have traveled all the way across Florida and are now heading for Miami once again.

The weather is so gorgeous for December seventeen and eighteenth. The temperatures are in the high sixties.

January fifth, two thousand seven. We cross over Couer D'Alene, Fourth of July, and Lookout Mountain. The scenery is beautiful but it has been snowing, adding to the already accumulation gathered on the mountain sides. The trees are white and the streams look black and cold below.

The plows have pushed the snow to the sides and caused a barrier from the steep drop. The cars don't seem to mind the conditions of the roads and speed by the truckers like they weren't there.

Snow Qualmie was shut down between I ninety and fifty nine while the avalanche patrol set charges to clear some of the snow to make the roads safer. Sand rather than salt is used on the mountain passes.

Wanting to go as far as possible we go as far as Livingston, Montana and park. The wind is so strong it rocks our forty two thousand pound load all night.

We have the strong wind behind us as we go over ninety east. They are drilling new oil wells in the area around Gillette, Wyoming.

We watch the many coal trains traveling across country and there are a lot of them.

We are nearing the Black Hills and hope to get over them before the storm that is building a head of us breaks. There is little snow, though we know South Dakota can have some vicious weather at anytime. We are heading over Sundonna to Spearhead, South Dakota. We are seeing more and more Mule deer. Not many horses out here.

We've had a little rain and snow as we come into Minnesota, Madison and Sun Prairie. Mostly clear roads into Illinois. We are heading for Watseka to drop our load and to pick up another and head for home. These eighteen wheels have seen a lot of territory in the last two weeks and are ready to be parked for a couple of days for a tune up.

We drop our load at the Big R just outside of Watseka and just kiddy corner across from it is a Big Rig grave yard. It seems strange to see those once beautiful tractors now at rest having given the highways all the miles they could. Like a heart transplant, those parts will keep another trucker going down the road.

On the road again, we make it out of North Carolina, South Carolina and Tennessee before the ice storm hit on January seventeenth of two thousand seven.

Black Mountain, Jellico, and the Smokies were good. There was quite a bit of traffic and good roads are what the truckers like.

I forty east. Check it out - Jellico Mountains, Great Smoky Mountains, long winding roads, long winding streams, Maggie Valley. All great places to see.

It's amazing how they built the roads in these mountains. I wonder what those road crews would have given then for the construction machines they have now. They had to be rough, tough men to endure what they did.

February first, two thousand seven. After eating breakfast at Beto Junction, Kansas we decided to take thirty five west to San Antonio, Texas. We watched the small white moon with the circle around it become a bright, large and orange as it slowly sank behind the hills.

I've been told that a circle around the moon means a change in the weather. I have only seen a circle around the moon once before. There were two at that time and by morning we had so much rain it flooded the camp ground we were once at in Wisconsin.

We hit a bad drop as we came to a bridge at Florence City limit and the road was so full of pot holes we almost bounced out of our seats. Thank goodness for seat belts.

With so much traffic across America I'm surprised they're not worse.

We delivered potatoes at Pearsal, Texas. It was an interesting operation the way they cut their seed potatoes.

We picked up a load of cabbage in crates and shrink wrapped. It is vegetable time out here. It's what keeps us moving.

Idle-aire, ten dollar member ship, two dollars an hour. Their claim is they will be in every truck stop, Wal-Mart distribution centers, warehouses, rest areas and so on. You not only pay two dollars a night, you pay for whatever other services you want from Idle-aire.

Idle-aire is alright in the summer-time if you don't have air conditioning or television in your truck. It's a high cost type of entertainment or getting a place to park in a truck stop.

It seems like a lot of things are being pushed down a truck drivers throat and taking more out of their wallets but not putting more into it.

Driving seventy north we listen to a great country station. Cowboy one-one-nine-o. Great songs. It follows us into Oklahoma.

Back home we listen to another great western oldies program from Waupaca, Wisconsin. Brought up with country music such as the Grand Ole Opry it can't be beat. The way they dressed when they presented themselves to the public couldn't be beat. The singers of today are alright but they dress in rags, have sex, show off their bodies thinking that's what people want. Where is the surprise any more when a young couple gets married? It shows no respect for themselves or anyone else.

We use to love watching GAC and C M T but not for a long time now. The academy awards use to be great but we can't stand that any more either.

The ice storm that hit Oklahoma left a devastating effect on homes and trees.

February twentieth, around Elkhart, Indiana in the evening we met up with fog so thick you couldn't see a foot ahead of you. Traffic was very cooperative for at least a hundred miles.

A young truck driver was very helpful in helping us find where we needed to go. Heading out of Kendalsville we still had fog for a long way, but not as bad.

Stopping at a T A the pot hole yard was still a back breaker as are the pot holed highways. Except for the pot holes and bad bumpy roads, we are enjoying this February twenty first with sunshine and a warm day after the bitter cold that hung on so long.

Going across South Dakota you begin to wonder if they are going to outdo Minnesota in the number of ponds and lakes. They have so much water standing around. So many fields with water where they don't need it. The cattle don't seem to mind as they cool their heels in it.

The corn is about three feet high in Georgia.

Peaches, Pecans, and other products are ready to be hauled. Good time of the year for the truckers.

Bill is yawning and making noises like he is tired or bored. More than likely bored. We will be able to park earlier tonight though and maybe get in a card game. Bill usually beats me. The cards aren't usually good to me when were on the truck.

I do better at home when we play cards with our friends, John and Bernice. John tells me I cheat but I'm just a better card player than he is or I have better cards. I usually get the cards he needs which makes me happy because Bernice gets the cards Bill needs. We joke around a lot but have a good time.

We don't take much time off but when we do we try to spend it with family for cook outs, Birthdays and other Holidays.

One of the things we don't like about Georgia is the dirty little Love Bugs "as they call them". What a nuisance they are. They are hard to get off the windshields.

You might say they are almost as bad as the Lake Flies that are so pesky in Wisconsin. Coming past a large body of water one night, Bill hit a large swarm of them and had a terrible time seeing to get to a gas station to scrub them off. They are so greasy and they are very hard to get off.

When we got to the company yard they couldn't believe the mess they made. I guess every state has something.

We went home and got caught up on a few things and Bill got his hours back so we can travel again.

Oranges are being hauled by the truck loads. But we are heading for Fort Lauderdale for a load of Salmon to take to Illinois.

The Ship was suppose to be in Friday but I guess the salmon was coming on what they call a slow boat from China. We finally do get our load though.

We pass a truck going sixty eight miles per hour down highway ninety five, weaving, but it's no wonder, he's trying to drive and work on his lap top also. I guess they can get away with it though. Just like wearing flip flops or if you're on crutches or you're so huge you can barely squeeze into your truck.

As we get closer to Fort Lauderdale the smoke is thick for a ways. But it's just a small contained brush fire. Thank God! We have seen the damage so many fires have done.

Picked up our load of Salmon and are on our way to Illinois to deliver it.

June eighth, had a load of potatoes to deliver in Ohio. It just had to be there but when we got to Zanesville we sat for four hours waiting to get unloaded.

June, two thousand seven. I call this the year of the corn. It seems everyone is raising corn for the ethanol fuel boom. Perhaps it's alright but like everything new we are inclined to ask, what will be the health risk from it?

We thought we had a good thing going with our trade with China. But we're finding out differently.

Lead in children's jewelry and toys. Poisons in food that is traded and now sheet rock that is used in our homes and makes people sick so they cannot live in them.

They say it's cheaper to get our products from other countries because they can make them cheaper. But is it worth it at the price of our children, pets and loved ones?

June twenty-nine, two thousand seven.

We stop at a grocery warehouse to have our load of canned stuff unloaded. They are outrageous in their Lumper fee of three hundred dollars. The most Bill has ever paid in the thirty five years he has driven truck is one hundred and twenty dollars. Our appointment was for six O'clock but were still sitting here at nine thirty. But they have their money.

Sometimes we sit for four to eight hours. It doesn't seem to matter if we have another pick up. Wal-Mart is also bad in that way.

At B and G at La Verngie, there is hardly any place to get in or out or back up to a dock. It's so dirty around the place and it stinks. This is a grocery warehouse.

Natures greenery. Going down highway one fifty one through Iowa everything is so beautifully green. The rolling hills are covered with corn fields and hay. From some hills you can see for miles. What a sight for the eyes.

Green is not just the color of money, it's Mother Natures' summer blanket, or should I say quilt with the color of the golden oats and wheat adding their patterns and the grey and black of the highways mingled in.

Colors of homes and flowers sprinkled in here and there. Rivers and lakes and streams make their own designs and the sun adds sparkles reflecting off the water.

Going across Kansas once again the water is so muddy and moving fairly fast in ditches and fields and streams. Flooding is taking its toll on crops. Oklahoma has its share and it looks like the rains are coming in again for Texas on this July second.

We are at a truck stop just inside of Texas and they sure don't need more rain. The huge pot holes are full and you drive through them very carefully. Some roads are still closed and the rivers are flowing fast and muddy and it continues to rain.

Closer to Winnsboro things are better. It is a little muddy but not near as bad.

The Truck stops are really bad. Bathrooms are dirty, lots of times no toilet paper, no paper toweling, no fans that work in the showers. Where are the employees? Where is the management?

One of my biggest beefs eating in some restaurants is when people get done eating and the waitresses clear off the table, they will wipe off the seat with the same cloth they wipe the table off with.

Do they not realize what some of those clothes touch before they sit on those seats? They touch the toilet seats, the floors, and the seats of the trucks that some drivers have dogs in and some of those trucker's clothes are not the cleanest.

We have seen men come in with their pants hanging down so their cracks show when they sit down on these very seats that the waitresses wipe off with the same cloth they wipe the table that we eat off from. Yuk! WE have complained but it does no good and when it happens a second time we do not go back there.

July fifth - Interstate Warehousing on I sixty five in Indiana is about the easiest place to find. We had a ten O'clock appointment but was at the dock by seven forty five and unloaded by eight o'five. There were three trucks ahead of us but all were loaded and gone. Very efficient place. Very neat.

RV'S, eighteen wheelers and four wheelers hum on down the highway. Better music than some they have on the radios.

Bill and a friend "Vern" tell of a waitress waiting on them and a couple of other friends. She asked what they'd like and one of them and his wife said a glass of water.

Without waiting for the rest of them to tell what they wanted she went and got their water. When she came back Bill said he would like one too. She got his and then Vern said he would also like. She made another trip and got his and then took their order.

When they were finished eating they left her a penny. As they walked out the door they heard the penny hit the door. They got a big laugh out of it. I don't think the waitress did.

Another story Bill tells (which is true) is how when Vern tried to make a phone call. He had to give a pass word to the operator. They were at a dock and he kept telling her D and she couldn't understand it. Finally he said Dum, Dum. Then she got it and Vern got the name of Dum, Dum.

Looking at the things in the truck stops, almost everything I picked up was made in China. What's the matter with American made things? It seems everything we buy now is made in a foreign country. Isn't it time to take back "our country"?

Can't we make our own products, run our own businesses? Do we realize what's happening to our country? Are we not the United States of America, or have we become the Foreign United States. That sure doesn't sound right to me. Our great grand children won't know who this Country belongs to if we let things keep on the way they are. I pray to God we wake up soon, for now I believe we are a "Blind America".

October eleventh, two thousand six. How ironic that five years and one month later another airplane hits a high rise in New York. No terrorist attack this time, but enough of a reminder of the first time that it had people running scared.

The small plane owned and flown by Lyle Corey crashed into it on a sightseeing tour. What an awful feeling to see that happen. Corey and his three companions were killed. He was a pitcher for the New York Yankees. Our sympathy goes out to all the families.

Going down highway forty one north near Fond Du Lac, Bill tries straddling a blown tire which he can't miss because it is all over the road and there was traffic on both sides of the semi.

The pieces of tire caught the trailers air hose and broke one. The busted air line caused the brakes to lock up and we left black marks for a half mile until we got stopped.

A driver in a pickup saw what happened and stopped and helped Bill wrap the hoses together to get us to Mack Truck garage just up the road.

The air hose let go before Bill got the truck in the yard with the eight flat tires. Mack got us fixed up enough to get us back to the home yard. Bill was grateful to the driver who stopped and helped him.

At Montrose we met two very nice waitresses. Though they were very busy, they took time to talk a few minutes with every one they waited on. They lit up the room with their smiles.

Bill was still tired from his four drop trip on Monday and they could see that but they had him cheered up before he left the restaurant.

One of the waitresses had worked a twelve hour split shift the day before and was back again for her regular shift. The other waitress came in at four thirty AM to work her shift until one-o'clock. The atmosphere of the place was very cheerful.

We are going to Parachete, Colorado and then back over the mountains on east seventy. They are such a rare scene I really enjoy them and the rivers and tunnels add to the beauty of them. Fishermen and rafters are enjoying another beautiful day.

At Montrose we met a very nice professional cowboy. He told us that he had fallen with his horse while rounding up some cattle and being as there was no one else around, he had to get back on his horse and find some help. He had pulled some tendons in his shoulder and broke his collar bone. Ouch! He looked like the professional cowboy he was.

He had worked the cattle from Texas, Georgia, Wyoming, Colorado and other states. He had been a truck driver for a few years but gave it up to pursue what he loved the most. We tried to encourage him to write a book. Perhaps in his older years he will.

Bill tells of going across the bridge near the Canyon River camp grounds when the snows had melted on the mountains and the water came to just below the bridge.

To keep from losing the bridge, a back hoe was used to keep the debris away from it. This was on I Seventy where they dug a channel for the water to go.

Bill was one of the last ones to be allowed to go through down town on main street of Salt Lake City on eighty nine as the snow melt rushed through the City. What a challenge that must have been for the men trying to keep the bridge from washing away and saving lives as well.

July thirty first, we are in the middle of the mountains loading at a chemical plant while train cars are sitting on several tracks waiting to be loaded. We go check our load on the scales and are on our way. The area is very secure and very neat.

Between Parachette and Rifle they are doing some major oil drilling. Since oil has gone higher, we were told they can now afford to build new refineries. Great! Perhaps gas prices will come down and people can afford to enjoy life a little more. It seems like so much has been taken away from us.

We are on the original road closer to the Colorado river. They have more or less hung another bridge a little higher. The original lower bridge is more scenic.

Some of the tunnels we go through are quite long and dark. As we go over Vail at ten thousand feet mark, my ears click and I move over toward Bill. We come to some areas where a person can see way down and there is no rail.

There are a few trucks and a motor home over heated and sitting on the side of the road. You've got to watch your speed going down these steep grades.

We have a weight of forty five thousand on so we travel at twenty five to thirty five MPH.

Due to a back up on Brecking Ridge Mountain we can't get our RPM's up to keep going, so we stop long enough to get them up again and be on our way. We are okay going through the Johnson Tunnel, which was built in nineteen seventy nine.

The Eisenhower Tunnel is just the other side and built in nineteen seventy three. They are both quite long.

We have one more mountain to go over and just as high and it will bring us into Denver. We look down into the valley of Georgetown where the homes are so crowded together near the mountain.

Heading for Ogallala, Nebraska the fog is thicker than pea soup. We are hauling Sodium Bicarbonate. A product mixed with cattle feed to keep them from bloating. It is like people taking a teaspoon of baking soda for an upset stomach.

The sun is coming out so it will soon burn the fog off.

On August first two thousand seven, the bridge over the Mississippi River on thirty five west in Minneapolis collapsed killing several people and injuring many more.

In its collapse it sent many cars and other vehicles sixty four feet below into the river. The Minneapolis Twins held their ball game to keep the traffic from causing more problems for a few hours more. I believe the rescuers and the people handled themselves quite well.

What a horrific tragedy.

We are home again to catch up on some things and a much needed rest. We have a bar-b-q with our kids and Prudence is happy to have more room to run.

On the road again in Ohio it is so humid. We run the Rig Master at night so we can sleep. Maybe it will cool off a little as we are now getting rain. But when the rain stops it will probably be just as humid and it looks like it is going to rain all day. Traffic is slow as it rains so hard, it's like a Monsoon. It is so dark, cars and trucks are stopping along the highway. Water is getting heavy on the highway and we are now having lightning and thunder with the rain.

We are almost to Cleveland and here we will fill up our truck and our tummies to give us a break from the storm.

No matter how wet the flag is, it's still true to its colors and keeps on flying. It has become quite windy now.

We are seeing cars and trucks in the ditch. We are down to about twenty miles an hour and it's not getting any better.

An accident ahead of us has traffic backed up. Road rage comes into the picture once again with foul language and threats to do one another in. Thank goodness they're in a back up and can't use their trucks. It would have to be fists. What immaturity. They shouldn't even be allowed to be in a truck.

When I think of how these drivers react to a situation like a back up makes me wonder what the future generation of truck drivers will be like when they have to take orders from their dispatchers and brokers. Especially when they are more or less bringing themselves up now without any one to answer to but their own selves.

These are our men and women of tomorrow who will be running our country. Perhaps it is time to bring back the draft to teach our young people what discipline and respect are. It shames me to see how our young people are allowed to dress and act in public.

It is still raining here in Austenburg but not as bad. On highway ninety east and west we come across a bridge near Harbor Creek, Pennsylvania that was rotting away so bad, we hope were not on it when it goes down. It is rusting so bad under-neath that most people wouldn't notice how bad it is.

There are so many bridges in New York that I wonder how long they will stand before they will collapse with the weight of eighty thousand pound trucks going over them every day. It's not just New York, other states have their share of bad bridges also. We are behind a car carrier loaded with cars and it is so rusty you wonder how the DOT can allow it.

We sleep at a rest area close to James Town. We had a terrible thunder and lightning storm and it felt like it shook the earth up pretty good. It is still lightening pretty good as we head down the road at six o'clock. It finally breaks around seven o'clock and it would have been nice to sleep through it but these eighteen wheels and the road calls us.

Going back to the yard, the manager came out to talk to us. "Wow!" I said, has any one told him that he was a double for Vince Gill? He said a woman in a gas station told him her heart nearly stopped when he walked in the door and she thought - Oh my God! It's Vince Gill. What a thrill that would have been to meet the real person. I have always been a great fan of his.

Bill tells me a story of his mother. Bill and his Mother were watching a fourth of July parade. The sun was hot and he took off his straw hat and put it on his mother's head. When they got home his mother took the straw hat off and she was speckled where the sun had come through the holes in the hat onto her face. She looked like she had the measles.

Bill's parents and grandparents were fairly tall but his grandmother was a short woman. Bill and his twin sisters must have taken after her as they were all three short. About five foot six. I guess his older son Mike took after his grandparents. His two younger ones were around Bill's height.

We are now at Bismarck, South Dakota at a truck stop and it is full. A lot of truckers are waiting for a load. Usually they don't have to sit long and we can tell when their orders come as they hurry through their breakfast and dash for their truck, happy to be on their way again. We were lucky as we had one for Spokane, Washington for Monday morning.

As we travel I-ninety four west the wheat fields are golden. The combines have been busy reaping the golden grain and large round bales of straw lay waiting to be hauled to the farm yard or where ever they'll take them.

From the wheat fields we pass fields of yellow Sunflowers with their bent heads facing East. The delicate bright yellow petals surround the dark brown center of seeds. They are a pretty sight to see.

Stopping at Painted Canyon we can view the scenic colors and formations. A very interesting place to visit and travel through.

We come across more fields of golden wheat and some sugar beet fields.

It seems a long way across Montana to Idaho but we have a beautiful day.

This is our second trip across Bitterroot, Pipestone, Homestake, Lookout and Fourth of July Mountains. We look out over the valleys below. Homes built on the high hills draw our attention.

The blue of the sky seems to touch the earth.

"This is Montana"

It's a beautiful place to visit or to live. A-A-A-H! A place of peace and serenity. Bill likes it as much as I do.

Big Wheels Rolling is being played on the radio and the words are so true of Bill and other dedicated drivers. I guess when you're young and you see those big trucks rolling down the highway you wonder what it's like to be so far off the ground looking down at all those little four wheelers and being able to see over the tops of them.

I wondered that for years until I met Bill and finally got my chance to experience it. It was a big thrill for me and I learned a whole lot about what the truckers go through every day there on the road.

As I've said before it really takes a very dedicated wife and family to understand the life of a trucker. And to stand by him and be there for him when he comes home from the road.

Bill has quit about five times, but that ole semi road bug just gets the best of him. I tell him that I'm going to have him given a blood transfusion so the doctors can take all those minute semis out of his blood. Each time he says he is retiring and we clean the truck out, I pack the things we always use in the truck and mark it. Because I know it won't be long and that ole bug will bite him again.

A sign along the highway reads Jesus is Lord of this Valley. I like to think he is Lord of all of this world.

Ninety West, the smoke is so thick as we come through mountains where a fire has burned acres and acres and left a long trail of charred black land. The smoke has drifted far west and as we travel through it, it burns the throat.

We are one hundred eighty miles from Coeur D' Alene which will take us into Idaho.

Bills favorite traffic is going by, the big ole train.

After getting a load out of Appleton, Wisconsin Bill headed for the highway. Going one way, there sat a train. He took another way and there sat another train or the same one that was a long one. So he figured he would take another route and dammed if there wasn't another train blocking his way. Thank goodness it didn't take the train long to move though. We had a good laugh over that.

Another fire closer to Missoula has burned more acreage and the smoke hangs heavy in the mountains and over the towns. The lookouts are busy today.

We follow the Coeur D' Alene lake for a while. The water is so clear and blue, speed boats and sail boats are being enjoyed on it.

Since we left Wisconsin I don't believe we've seen any lakes or streams as bad with algae as they are in Wisconsin. I wonder what the other states secrets are. What a shame to let our natural resources go to hell. But like our bridges we have a tendency to ignore what is so valuable to us.

August thirteen, two thousand seven, Bill's birthday. This is the age he wanted to retire but I can't tell what age it was because he still wants to drive.

How do you celebrate a birthday on a semi? Of course there are ways but I won't tell. Go figure.

We drop our load of paper products and head for a truck stop. We are on a seven percent grade. Didn't notice it last night in the dark but then you don't notice a lot of things in the dark.

It is about fifty three degrees at five fifty six in the morning in Spokane, Washington.

August fourteenth, again we are sitting here waiting for a load. There are many drivers in the same boat.

It's Wednesday the fifteenth and we're now leaving Spokane. This is reefer and flatbed country. We are getting a load of cardboard out of Wenatche to haul to Minnesota.

We watch the dust devils as they move across the fields blowing things out of their way. They can be pretty vicious and you don't want to be caught in their path.

This reminds me of a poem someone sent to me when I was about sixteen. It goes like this:

> A little wind went whirling far across the land
> Sent the leaves a swirling high above the sand
> But it stopped to whisper as it passed me by
> I was once a whirl wind, now I'm just a sigh.

There is more to it but I don't remember it, and I never did find out who sent it.

Heading toward Wenatchee we see fields and fields of vineyards, fruit trees of peaches, apples and so on.

The water coming over the Rock Island Dam is so white it looks frozen. We cross the Rock Island River which is so long and blue.

I wonder if this is where Johnny Cash got his idea for his song. In Indian language Winatchee means 'Man's many knives' or 'Lot of water'.

It is really interesting to go down I-ninety and be able to tell what crops are being raised in the fields. Potatoes, cornfield grain, corn, grass, hay, wheat, peppermint and sugar grass. There are signs for a long way telling what the crops are. There are so many other crops I wished I knew the names of.

We are back in Idaho crossing the Couer D' Alene Lake. It continues through the Idaho panhandle forest which goes over the Fourth of July Mountains, which is a six percent grade.

Bill is yawning and of course it's catching. He had a good night and he is starting to relax as we are taking a few months off soon. From the Fourth, we go to Lookout again. It seems so much steeper this time.

Going over these mountains reminds us of when we went over Donner Pass and we had to put chains on. We got them laid out, ready to put them on when the sign lit up telling us we didn't need them. I grabbed mine up and gave them to Bill to put away.

There is construction work going on, on Lookout so our mileage is down.

August eighteenth, floods, mud slides, roads washed out, railroad bridge washed out, more people killed in Minnesota and Wisconsin near La Crescent, La Cross and Winnona. Hurricane in Hawaii, Earth quakes in Peru and flooding in Texas. What is disrupting our planet so bad?

A few years back Bill was driving down the highway at his regular speed and there was quite a bit of traffic. A young man tried to pass him and Bill wouldn't let him because of the traffic conditions. The young man became very angry and pulled up beside Bill. When Bill pulled over to the side of the road, the young man jumped out of his car and Bill looked at him and pointed down the road to where the young man's car was going with his baby daughter in it.

Road Rage! It doesn't pay.

Hurricane Francis is being felt across the U.S. as we travel from ninety to thirty five to eighty five west across Iowa, Nebraska and Wyoming going into Utah, Nevada and our destination California.

The wind and rain are hitting us with a temperamental force.

As we roll across Wyoming we see snow on Elk Mountain on this wet and windy Labor Day weekend.

A lot of beef cattle are cleaning up their act after going without a shower for a while.

Our windshield has been thoroughly washed after being covered with bugs. Thank goodness the cold weather will soon take care of them even though I hate to see the cold weather come.

A large black cloud greets us as we come over a hill and it looks like we're going into a tunnel. I ask Bill if he thinks there's a light at the end of the tunnel. There was and the sky became brighter for a while.

We don't see any deer but the antelope are still playing out here.

The wide open spaces makes Wyoming a tremendous playground. What a beautiful place to play.

Casper, a small town, is an interesting place with its old time scenario. We had a pick up there but sat for two and a half days waiting for it because there was a holiday being celebrated. We walked around the small town and bought a few things at a vegetable and fruit stand. There wasn't much to see otherwise.

We hauled Bentonite out of there that is used in oil wells and keeping medicines and certain foods soft.

Outside of Wright, Wyoming we saw one of the largest herds of Buffalo we've ever seen. They didn't seem to be distracted by all the traffic going by.

As we traveled toward Rock Springs I could picture the Indians of long ago living along the rocky cliffs and hunting the wild animals for food and clothing.

The cuts in the rocks and the weather must have destroyed many of the old cliff homes. Looking at the formations that are left behind is an interesting sight and you can use your imagination to no end. What a heritage we have. "History", what would we do without it!

There is so much to see and learn as to how our country evolved since the time God created this huge Universe to what we have now.

Just think, even these big trucks are a part of our history.

The trucking industry started out with someone delivering products from one town, city or even another state with horse and wagon because some store needed something and they didn't have the means of getting it themselves.

And then came the trains and bigger trucks and faster service. Just stop and think how the mail service got started and how it has progressed through the centuries.

Planes and big trucks do the bulk of seeing that our mail gets through. Trains and ships and big trucks see that our products keep America growing. We also have the people who deliver many of our smaller products to out of the way places or to businesses who need an item now from across town or another distant city.

In some way we all help keep America moving and that is all a part of making history.

There is so much to see. The Tetons, Yellowstone, Old faithful, and so much more.

Taking nineteen at Rocks off from eighty will bring you into Yellowstone which is at the corner of Wyoming and Montana. The Rocky Mountains are quite the sight as they are covered with snow.

The Unita Mountains take you into Echo Canyon. Part of where the Anasazi and Fremont Indians and other Tribes lived.

Just out of Echo Canyon we can see Devils slide. It is etched with silver rock from the peak to the highway. To slide down would sure take care of the hemorrhoids. Ouch!

The trains are running alongside the highways or winding their way through the mountains. Sometimes two to five engines pulling, depending on what their hauling. Coal, scrap, gravel, vehicles, ETC.

The colors are coming out on the trees adding to the beauty of the mountains. Beautiful herds of horses can be seen grazing in the pastures at the foot hills of the mountains.

There are crystal clear streams easy to get to for a good day of fishing. The Rain Gods have been good this year for the streams are full and the water swift. This is all a small part of America. Tour it and see what our men and women are fighting to protect and keep free.

There is a story told of two Indians, Running Bear and Falling Rock. To decide who was to become Chief of their Tribe, they were sent out to see who could bring back the most food.

Running Bear came back after a month with Antelope, Deer and some smaller animals. Falling Rock never came back and to this day you see signs, 'Watch For Falling Rock'.

The Great Salt Lake. I have always enjoyed seeing that great body of white. Now when I see it and it has become an eye sore because thoughtless people who travel across there are throwing litter of beer bottles, soda cans, pieces of tires and other litter on to it. What a shame to destroy a piece of our history that way. What a shame we are becoming a society of no pride and no respect for our country.

Coming off from Monteagle we see signs for Ruby Falls. Although we were there several years ago we wonder if there have been any changes made. Not that there should be, unless it would be to make the paths wider to accommodate my expansion.

Crossing the great body of water of the Gulf Of Mexico, it is a sight to behold. The water is rough and black and clear of debris. A small boat is speeding across the choppy waves and a large plane is speeding across the grey blue sky.

It is eight O'clock in the morning and traffic is heavy. We dropped our load of paper at ST. Petersburg and are now heading toward Auburndale on I four.

Traffic going west on I four is backed up temporarily. New roads and bridges are being built and the whiteness of the cement slaps you in the face as the sun hits it. As with all construction it will be nice when it is done.

Everything is really green and it is quite a contrast to our own Wisconsin brown in this month of July.

Nineteen counties have been declared a disaster because of the heat. I guess we can look forward to this every year, only not so bad.

This is the year of two thousand six.

Florida has its own problems with fires just about every year and later, early frosts. Mother nature is not picky what she throws at our farmers.

We passed beautiful Lake Ariana Resort. The lake is blue and tranquil and no activity on it.

We pass acres of orange groves already picked. Having picked up part of a load of Orange Juice we head for Plymouth for another load to take to Michigan.

We take I four to east exit fifty five, highway twenty seven north to one ninety two east, four twenty nine north to four forty one north, Lakeview Drive to our destination in Plymouth.

That is quite a route and quite scenic. Someone said there used to be one hundred lakes in this area, but are now only sixty eight. Seems like the water tables are going down all over.

Just as we're about to leave our destination at Plymouth the wind comes up and makes a white out from the dust.

Looks like we are heading into another storm. Our third or fourth this week. Although we are loaded we can still feel the wind rock us. With Bill's experience with the wind and storms and driving over the roads these many years, he has pretty much everything under control. But he also knows to expect the unexpected.

As we traveled down the highway we'd reminisce about Bill's younger trucking days and some of his trucking experiences or he would talk about his sons whom he was quite proud of. As he talked sometimes he would tear up because he hadn't spent enough time with them when they were younger. But I knew he did what he did because he wanted to give them a decent living.

It's too bad our children don't realize we can't always do what we'd like to for them. Sometimes it takes growing up to realize why our parents did what they did at the time. It doesn't mean they love you any less. If we look back at the circumstances we can realize it was for the better and we bettered ourselves because of it.

Bill is very proud of all three of his sons and what they have accomplished with their lives.

A truck driver's life is not his own and though Bill tried many other kinds of work so he could spend more time at home with his family his heart was always on the road but his thoughts were always on his family.

The split from the children's mother hurt him more than they will ever know.

Running trips to Milwaukee when he first started trucking he told how he would drop a load and then go back to Green Lake for another. He was short hauling two or three times a day. While they unloaded him he would try to catch upon some sleep.

Usually he was paid by the trips which was usually seventy dollars a day. Sometimes he worked six days a week.

Starting at two in the morning and worked until ten or eleven at night, he usually got about four or five hours of sleep and then went back at it again.

I guess when you're young and foolish and want the best for your family you do these things. You think your indispensable.

Like I said, we reminisced about his younger days.

He would tell about trying to get home to watch one of his sons wrestle in his school matches. He would always tell how good he was. It was always told with pride.

Bill tells of another son who sold his car for a trip to California. He left in August from Wisconsin and went to Seattle, Washington to visit friends and then stayed in Florida for a short time. He then traveled highway one-o-one to San Diego, California. He sold his motorcycle to a friend there but drove it home and traded the cycle for his friends pickup.

We wonders if the memories come flashing back to him, reminding him of the great times he must have had. It really is great to be young.

We wonder what he would think of the changes after all these years were he to make the trip again with his family.

Back to basics. The long hard pull over Monteagle made the international hum. Other truckers had their four ways on showing caution to others.

There is not much conversation among the truckers when going down a mountain with a heavy load.

Going seventy five north we cut our speed to a slow pace as a pickup has hit a car, taking out the whole back end and damaged his hood.

In another accident a turkey hit a truckers windshield causing him to pause. Having one of those suckers hit you is like running into a wall.

Of course this brought out more stories. Like the trucker who had his windows open and an Owl flew in, flapping and attacking the driver.

The driver tried to subdue the Owl while at the same time trying to get the truck stopped and to get out. Opening the doors the Owl finally flew out. Though the driver was scratched up they were both glad to be rid of each other.

Another driver told of an eighteen wheeler parked just below a hill and a snowmobiler came over the hill and went through the windshield. I do not know where this took place as he did not say. He did not say how badly either one was hurt.

Coming down off the mountains on I sixty four east, I started looking, really looking at the map and at the mountains that practically surround West Virginia and Virginia.

Pennsylvania and Kentucky and Tennessee have their share also. They are intermingled and make for a scenic view. It is a beautiful sight in the fall also when the leaves all turn color.

The cuts in the rocks tell what a job it was to put roads through the mountains where no roads had ever been. The roads are quite curvy and you can't always see very far so you take it easy going down these mountains.

We come across I sixty four east to six sixty four south through a long tunnel and over a bridge crossing the Atlantic Ocean. What a sight. White caps stir the water and there are ships of all kinds sitting in the Harbor.

We are not too far from where my grandson Andrew spent four years in the Navy.

He has been out for about a year and the ironic thing is, he is out here on vacation visiting some Navy buddies. But we can't get together as Bill has a load to get rid of in the next city.

Eight twenty seven '06. Forty west toward Gallup, New Mexico we come across several miles of where there had been a mud slide. Trucks were busy scraping the mud off the highway and hauling it away.

The highways are alive with yellow flowers. Bill tells me this is New Mexico's rainy season.

Back tracking a bit to Moriarity, we see hundreds of prairie dogs. We watch them as their Sentries watch for danger of any kind.

Going into New Mexico reminds me of when Bill and I went to a race there and it was so dusty and as the cars went around the tracks the wind blew the dust our way.

When we got back to town we stopped at a restaurant to have a bite to eat before we went to our camper for the night. Going to the bathroom before we went home I glanced in the mirror and to my horror I looked like a Raccoon. I couldn't get out of there fast enough. It was then I realized why people had a silly grin on their faces in the restaurant.

I scolded Bill for taking me to the restaurant and not telling me how dirty my face was.

The storm that hit New Mexico, eight twenty one '06 sent mud over the road at the check point between Las Cruces and Deming, New Mexico, along highway ten west. The desert was flooded with water and is as green as we've ever seen it. Even the Rio Grande was full and they talked about evacuating a small place called Hatch which was nearby.

Some of the Arroyos are washing so bad they are becoming a hazard to the roads.

Traveling into Texas, the oil wells are pumping away. When you observe these big oil fields you wonder why there is a shortage of gas or diesel fuel.

As wet as New Mexico is, Texas is dry.

It is good to be traveling right along at seventy miles an hour legally and the cars at eighty. Traffic seems to be running smoothly, no backups, not much construction to hold a person up and no tolls. Roads are good, grass is kept mowed and no trash to speak of.

Just east of Abilene we come across two separate forest fires. So far they seem to be fairly well contained.

Nine one '06. At Carrolton we load up with ceramic tiles. We're light on the nose but hope with some more fuel we'll be alright. We then head for Frederick, Maryland to drop the load on Tuesday. Coming through the mountains of Virginia, they must be having trouble to get her to buckle up, because they have signs up telling her to buckle up.

Going north on eighty one there is a large semi turned on its side in the ditch. A mile further on another one lays on its side with the trailer split wide open.

About five or ten miles further there is another accident between two semis shutting eighty one south down and causing a backup of about ten or fifteen miles. It's times like these that truckers get angry if they have to be at a drop or pick up at a certain time. There is usually no place they can get out of their predicament and of course they are late for other drops or pickups or they lose them altogether which means a loss of money for them. That hurts.

Because of Labor Day weekend we stayed at Flying J in Maryland. Had supper and watched part of the races - Nascar. We always enjoyed them.

We were surprised when we left the restaurant to see two FEMA motor homes (the very expensive ones) sitting in the truck parking lot. Why were they here in Maryland and not in Mississippi or New Orleans.

Why the big expensive motor homes that cost a fortune when that money could have been helping the destitute families of Katrina. Does it really make sense?

The rain in Maryland is so heavy, it's almost like driving in fog. Some of the small cars are without lights and it makes it hard to see them. The lights on some are so small you can hardly see them when they are on. What a safety hazard!

We are heading for Pennsylvania with a load of steel strapping. They will get half of our load and Tomahawk, Wisconsin will get the other half.

Finally heading back to Wisconsin. Traffic is so heavy in Illinois. Of course all the construction work, school's out and people going home from or to work didn't help. It is expected in Chicago especially around the loop.

In September we take time off from driving. Bill has driven a good many miles throughout the years in the winter time and decides to take a break from the snowy roads.

He has taken a few other winters off when we were first married. We would take our Montana fifth wheel and head for Deming, New Mexico and camp at Sunrise Camp Ground.

We would connect up with friends who would also camp nearby in another camp ground. We would go rock hunting or visit a melting plant or old villages.

Bill and I visited an old Indian cave in the mountains. The trail we had to climb was very narrow and very scary. I imagine it was in better shape when the Indians used it. There has been hundreds of people who have climbed that path since they did.

It was very interesting the way they had that cave carved in the mountain. There were several rooms for the different families.

The ceilings were so blackened from their fires and there were no artifacts left there. It would have made it more interesting had there been.

Going down the other side of the mountain I didn't realize my shoe string had come untied and I stepped on it and almost fell, but Bill caught me.

We also visited White Sands. The Sand was so white and there were children with their flying saucers sliding down the hills of sand. Some would just roll down them and pick themselves up and brush off as the sand did not stick to them.

There is so much to see in each state of our U.S.A. What a wonderful country we live in. I pray to God we never let another person or country take it away from us. And I sincerely pray we never let anyone take our freedom from us.

Two thousand nine. Our economy is so bad. People have lost their jobs, their homes and their health insurance. Food pantries can't keep up with the demand for food.

We have seen more rummage sales this year than ever before. People are trying to keep their heads above water.

Shopping in the stores we watch what people buy and they are being very conservative. You can tell who has a job by what they buy and by who can afford to go out to eat in a restaurant.

It almost makes you envious or angry. Though we don't like it I feel we are learning to live a different kind of life. People are learning to grow their own food. Though there isn't enough space in the city to grow much. But, what we can, helps. Sometimes I wonder if God is trying to bring us to our knees and tell us something for we have gotten so far away from his teachings.

We have lost so much of our honor, respect, pride and love for our country.

People who do not believe in God. Those whom believe in Gay Marriages. Those whom do not believe in our flag. What's happened to our beloved America.

On Nine Eleven O One, the terrorists attacked the twin towers in New York, killing thousands of our innocent men, women and children. What a terrible tragedy that was. Flags were flown from almost every vehicle, business and home.

Our young men and women were sent to Iraq to fight these terrorists. Giving their lives to save ours. Many came back maimed and with other problems.

Where are the flags to show our support? What? Shouldn't they be remembered every day of their life and beyond? Have we forgotten?

Bill and I traveled through about twenty states about a year after the attack, stopping in at least two truck stops a day. We looked and asked for flags to fly on our antenna of our truck. You guessed it. Except for two or three with the real little flags, they didn't carry them anymore. Oh yes, they had the stickers. We bought some of them and put them on our windows.

We know the cloth flags do not last long flown on the antenna of these big rigs, but we especially wanted to fly one for the week leading up to Memorial weekend and as long as the flag would last.

Though our little flags don't last long, Old Glory will last forever.

There will always be truck drivers to deliver our products, and there will always be brave men and women to fight for our freedom and we should not let those who have a mind to destroy our beloved country do it!

Bill and I

The squeaky cart could be heard going up and down the grocery store aisles. It ground on the nerves and I tried to ignore it. "Why would the stores keep those carts when they don't work right?" I mused, feeling irritated.

I turned down another aisle to get away from it but then I heard it coming right behind me.

I tried turning down another aisle and as I did, I left my cart long enough to get a jar of peanut butter.

There was a loud bang and I turned just in time to see this elderly, grey haired man pull his cart away from mine, with a smile on his face.

"Sorry lady," he replied, "guess I wasn't looking where I was going."

"No I guess you weren't." I replied, giving him a stern look.

Grabbing my cart I started away from him, only to hear him following me.

Thinking I would stop and let him pass, he stopped along side of me. He stood looking at me and as I was about to move away he asked me if I was going to apologize?

"What?" I gasped.

"You ran into me." he replied.

"Why you---." I stuttered.

Before I could answer he handed me a card and said if you want to write me an apology, here's my address and my page number.

"Of all the nerve." I thought. "Never!"

I scrunched it up and gave it a toss into my cart, as he walked away grinning.

"June," I heard him call. "Are you ready to go?"

"June," I wondered, "was that his wife or girl friend? And he expected me to call or write him. What was he, a Jig-a Lo?"

As I took the groceries out of the bags when I got home, I was surprised to find the scrunched up note in one of the bags. I left it there as I folded the bags and put them away between the refrigerator and the cupboard.

Living with my daughter Beth at the time, I kept busy with doing things around the house and with my grandsons, Andrew and Eric.

My daughter worked nights and I didn't mind the house work.

I didn't think about the man in the store or his note again until my daughter found it in one of the bags I had stored away.

"Mom," she called, "what is this card from?"

I took a look at it and explained about it.

"He claimed I ran into him." I said.

"When did this happen?" She asked.

"Just before Christmas," I replied. "I'm surprised it's still around."

"Mom, maybe it's a sign."

"You got to be kidding!" I exclaimed.

So Beth said, "I think you should call or write to him."

"Oh for Petes sake. I thought I threw that away. Throw it in the garbage."

"Why should I apologize to him? He ran into me and besides, he was with another woman. So he is probably married or she was probably his girl friend."

"I bet it isn't either one." She argued.

"Will you just throw it away?" I asked.

Two days later I found the note by my breakfast meal.

"Oh Shit." I mumbled.

Ready to toss it away, I thought maybe she's right.

I tried the number he had written on the card and got his answering machine.

When I heard his voice I became a little intrigued and I thought, "Oh well, maybe I'll try in a few days."

With Beth's coaxing I tried another number he had written on the card.

"Hello," came the voice, "Sunset Campground."

That couldn't be Bill, I thought. He sounds different.

"What can I do for you?" Asked the voice?

"Do you know how I could get in touch with Bill Schoen?" I asked. "He gave me a note and asked me to call him."

"Well ma'am, Bill went to Michigan about two weeks ago and he didn't say when he'd be back."

"Well just tell him the lady he ran into with his cart in the grocery store in Wisconsin called. But not to apologize."

Hard telling what he's doing in Michigan, I thought as I hung up, feeling embarrassed. Then I remembered June.

"Did you get hold of him?" My daughter Beth asked.

"No!" I replied, "and I'm not calling him again. I think he's probably married to some person named June. I forgot about her and they've gone to Michigan.

Besides he must live in New Mexico somewhere at a campground.

What in the world would I do in New Mexico so far away from my family?"

We had a family of ten living in the lower apartment and for Christmas I made each of them a quilt.

Their mother home schooled them all. She had been a School teacher and was good at it.

In the spring two of the boys graduated from high school and went on to college in the fall.

After Christmas I kept myself busy with house work and my grandsons and writing stories.

My dream had always been to write and that winter I wrote three of them hoping to some day to get them published.

To my surprise, in March, I got a phone call from Bill. I didn't know how he knew my number, but found out Beth had called the campground a few days before and left my number with the man who had answered when I had called.

When I answered the phone, the first thing he asked me was if I was ready to apologize to him for running into him.

"No!" I exclaimed. "You ran into me. Any ways, why are you calling me? June probably wouldn't like it."

"June," he replied laughing, "She was just someone I took back to Wisconsin so she could spend Christmas with her family. She definitely is not my girl friend and I'm not married.

When I saw you in the store I wanted to meet you again, but didn't have time to talk. And you disappeared in a hurry."

"Well I didn't know you from Adam and how did you know if I was married or not? And how do you know if I am or not?"

"Because your daughter said you weren't when she left a message at the campground." He said.

"My daughter! OOOh shoot. She wasn't even suppose to call."

"So have you got time to talk now?" He asked.

I gave a deep sigh and said, "I guess so."

As it turned out, we talked for quite a while and my daughter would giggle every once in a while as she lay on the couch listening, even though she could only hear half of the conversation.

We talked about traveling and camping and both agreed we enjoyed it. And when I agreed it was always more fun when there were at least two, my daughter screamed out, "Mom!"

I started laughing because she didn't know what We were talking about.

Bill got the gist of it and we had a good laugh over it.

Over the next month we talked quite a bit and got to know each other better.

Sometime in May, Beth informed me she was taking a week's vacation and going to Oklahoma to visit a friend there. Her son Andrew was going with her and she asked if I would like to go along.

I always enjoyed traveling and took her up on the offer.

When Bill and I talked again I told him of our plans and he said he would like to meet me again and would it be alright if he came to Oklahoma.

We decided on a place to meet and Beth, her son and I got a room at the Motel Six. The first night there we didn't bother to ask about Bill because we were tired out from the long trip.

In the morning after breakfast, Beth and Andrew went to visit her friend and I inquired if they had a Bill Schoen registered there.

They checked their records and said no they didn't. I went back to my room and started reading to pass the time until Beth came back.

I checked once more on Bill but was told he hadn't come in yet. Beth and her son came back about three and we went sightseeing and had supper before we went back to the motel and played some cards, watched some TV and crawled into our beds.

Beth slept on the floor saying it was better for her back.

After another day and a "no show Bill" we did some more sightseeing and decided we'd leave the next day.

In the morning, Beth and her son went out to eat and to see her friend again.

I decided to stay at the motel in case Bill did show up. I cleaned the room and started packing our things when someone knocked on the door.

I peeked out to see a man standing there. I called through the door and asked what he wanted.

"I'm Bill," he replied, "I'm looking for Juanita."

I opened the door and stared at the white haired, elderly, good looking, slim man standing there with a smile on his face.

We talked for awhile and then before I knew it he had me in a bear hug.

"Gosh I'm glad to finally meet you again." He said.

I was embarrassed by the hug.

I told him we'd been there a couple of days and had checked for him several times but was told he was not there.

He was upset about it because he had inquired about us also and had been told we were not there either.

We stayed another couple of days and I got to meet Bill's miniature schnauzer, Prudence.

As we talked, he told me he had a chance to move a Veterinarian from New Mexico to Arizona. He asked if I would stay and go with him. Then we'd go back to New Mexico and get his trailer and go to Wisconsin.

I knew I had to stay with him because it was love at first hug. Beth was happy for me and liked Bill right away.

They headed back to Wisconsin as Beth's vacation was about over with and Andrew had to go back to school.

We had a good trip to Arizona and got the Veterinarian settled in before we went back to New Mexico. She paid all the expenses and was glad to be in her new place.

Bill and I stayed in New Mexico a couple of months in his trailer that he had in a trailer park. I really enjoyed our time there, getting to know Bill and his friends.

I believe the little schnauzer was a little jealous. After all, Bill belonged to her. But I tried to give her a lot of attention and sneak her a treat once in awhile.

I loved animals, but it still took Prudence and I awhile to feel comfortable around each other and for her to really trust me.

We would take her for walks and she would walk beside Bill. If she started to wonder away all Bill would have to do was to point his finger at her and show her where she was suppose to be, which was at his side and she would be there. If she wandered too far, he would clap his hands and she would come running back to him. She was a very well trained dog.

With the warmer weather, we decided to head for Wisconsin. Bill was not one to tolerate the cold weather.

We stayed at my daughter's place in the country for a few weeks and then moved on to Wisconsin Dells to a camp ground not far from his oldest son's place.

Bill's son, Mike, owned a paint ball business at his home and a place called Splatter Zone in the Dells. Mike and his friend Diane ran the business together for several years.

Being short of help that summer, Bill offered to help out and I started calling him a professional girl watcher. He would have been a good carnival barker.

While Bill helped his son, I took a job at a motel called Fields.

I had gone to seven other motels before going there. The other ones were all owned by foreigners and I was told they only hired their own people.

I worked with some very nice foreign students who were very good workers. They didn't have the best accommodations for living and I felt sorry for them because they were taken advantage of.

When they left in September, I knew I would miss them until they came back the following year. That was their last year they could come as they would graduate after they went back home and finished school. The Girls were then expected to get married and the boys had to go into the military for two years.

What I was told is that what our apartment complexes in the big cities look like, is what they lived in - in their country.

We kept in touch for the first year after they left and then the mail ended. I guess that was the way it was in Finland.

For the next couple of years, Bill helped his son out as I worked at the motel. Bill enjoyed his work at the Splatter Zone and could talk to anybody that came around. He had a knack for drawing people to the games and a sense of humor.

When Mike closed up shop the first year, Bill and I enjoyed ourselves looking in the stores and walking around town. On one of our walks, he turned to me and said he would be leaving for New Mexico soon. I just looked at him and waited for him to say something more.

After a few minutes, he took my hand and asked me if I would marry him. I figured it took him long enough to ask that question, but I answered "YES!" I was sure I wouldn't find another guy quite like Bill.

We set our wedding date for October second of nineteen ninety eight. We were married at the campground with my two sons - Jack and George giving me away and my daughter Beth as my Bridesmaid.

Bill's son Mike was his best man and his son Jay was our camera man.

The wedding dinner was held at Sandy's in Lyndon Station, Wisconsin with friends and relatives attending. We left for New Mexico soon after that in a hail of rice.

There was so much to do and see in New Mexico. Our neighbors next to us gave us a welcome back dinner and were happy we had gotten married. We didn't do much together as Connie was not a well person. But we were able to visit with her husband Bob and their dog "Puppy".

Puppy wanted to be friendly but if we got too close to him he would hide behind Bob. If we had a treat for him he would poke his head around Bob and take it and then dash behind him again like a shy child.

Bill and I made new friends in the park. With them and our previous friends we did a lot of sightseeing together.

We took in a tour of a large smeltering plant and were engrossed with the colors of the metal as it melted and ran into large vats. Other days we took rides to old battle grounds and walked through the fields where there were still signs of the battles that had taken place so many years ago.

When I was in school and read about these things, I had been interested in it but it did not impress me that much. But having seen some of the effects of these wars that took so many of our young people and comparing them to what our soldiers have to fight with today, I wonder how any of them survived.

I am in great awe of them and of our fighting men and women today.

We went rock hunting in caves and found some turquoise and a few other precious stones. Walking down the path to leave I looked down and found a fossil rock. It had the imprint of a fern like plant and other imprints on it and it made my day.

Besides finding the fossil, something else that struck me as really fantastic was visiting an old stone church in Hachita, New Mexico, just off of highway nine and forty six.

The front of the church was made of stone and glass as was the burial place of the Priest who had preached at that church for many years. They buried the Priest under about five feet of concrete so no one could move him.

As we went into the church, it brought back many memories of Jesus' birth and death. The seven or eight foot colorful statues that stood in the wall depicted every stage of our saviors death. It is unbelievable to see such a beautiful display, but sad.

There was so much to see and do while we were in New Mexico and we had a great time.

On Sundays after church and lunch, we would go to the campground just down the road from ours and listen to the polka band play. A young woman of ninety one would dance just about every dance. And if she could find a dance in town anywhere, she was there dancing up a storm. It was hard to believe she was ninety one.

As the weather warmed, we were all ready to head back to Wisconsin or our various homes. Wayne and Mary Jane would miss their hills and trails they liked to climb or walk.

We knew Tony and Sylvia would miss their playing with the Polka band and their other friends. But we all promised to keep in touch.

Heading home, Bill became quiet and I knew something was on his mind. But I waited for him to say something. After a few minutes he looked at me with a serious look on his face and I knew something was up.

Bill and I could almost read each other's thoughts.

"Well," I said, "you may as well tell me what's on your mind."

I had a pretty good idea what it was.

"What would you think of me going back over the road?"

"I wouldn't care but I'd get awful lonesome without you." I replied.

"Oh, I wouldn't think of going without you coming along." He replied. "I would have to find a job where you could ride too."

I had always wondered what it would be like to ride in one of those trucks that seemed like it was a mile above me when I was in the car passing one of them.

"Okay." I said.

With time off now and then, Bill had driven truck for more than thirty years when we met.

Bill didn't have any trouble finding a job and we checked the truck over good to make sure we didn't have to spend a lot of time cleaning the inside of it. While it was fairly clean we scrubbed it with Lysol.

After a few weeks of sleeping in it we bought a new mattress and a sponge mattress for the top of it. It was quite comfortable after sleeping on the old one.

It was amazing what we could get along without. Besides the bunks, we had a closet we used for our clothes and another one we put shelves in for our medication, a few groceries, cleaning supplies and various other things we would need while living in the truck.

We had a couple of plastic drawers we put our under things and writing material in. I would continue to write while on the truck.

I also took books along to read, word puzzles and embroidery to have something to do while Bill drove.

While he did the logs to keep track of all his stops and loads, fuel and in bunk time, I kept track of our routes and what we picked up and a few other things.

It seemed we had quite a few night drops which were hard because we were in strange cities and it wasn't easy reading some of the signs, especially at night. There were several times we got lost and had to back track.

If we took a wrong turn in the daytime, we at least saw some beautiful country.

Taking a wrong turn once we wound up going down a rancher's private road lined with a white fence. The horses grazed nearby but didn't pay any attention to our big rig as it went by. But evidently, someone did as when we looked in our mirrors, a police officer was behind us and followed us out and off of the rancher's land.

I wondered if he knew we were lost. He didn't bother us. Most often Bill knew the routes pretty good.

It amazed me how he could remember some of the places, but then he had been over these places hundreds of times. He could still tell me of places he'd been, what he delivered to the various places.

He has an amazing memory and he had some great people to work for and he enjoyed the jobs.

Sometimes we'd just reminiscence about Bill's life before I met him.

He was born in the small town of Baraboo, Wisconsin and lived there until he was nineteen years old.

Though Bill wasn't involved in sports in school, he liked to play softball with boys around the neighborhood.

He enjoyed going roller skating with friends Harlan, Jimmy, Norman and several others.

When Bill was small, his mother would take him and his twin sisters fishing just to spend time alone with them.

His mother worked in the Powder Plant where they made explosives for a number of years. The Powder Plant was open for fifty or sixty years and employed many people. Today it stands empty and in ruins.

When World War II ended in nineteen forty five, there was a large parade for the soldiers and they marched proudly down the streets of Baraboo.

It was a scene I witnessed several times and though I was only thirteen, I knew it was a very special day for everyone, especially our men and women in uniform.

Today we still honor those same men and women in our parades and in our thoughts.

Bill's father managed a gas station and worked as a Bartender and clean up man at the Bar-B-Q near the swimming pool on business twelve.

The Bar-B-Q was built in nineteen thirty seven. Besides serving beer, there was also a soda bar and a bowling alley. There was also a bar in the basement with a dance floor.

At the age of twelve, Bill started staying with his Aunt Rose and Uncle Everett "Eve" helping them out in the summer time with chores and in the pea fields. He would have to get up early in the morning to get the barn chores done and then head out to the pea fields.

They would take the peas to the pea vinery where they were shucked out and picked up and taken down to the cannery.

This work lasted about two weeks, but there was other work to keep him busy.

Bill's twin sisters helped around the home. Like a lot of families, Bill and his sisters had their problems and Bill being the oldest, took the blame for a lot of things and so he spent a lot of time on the farm.

As he grew older he helped his father at the gas station he managed. In those days you pumped the gas, washed the windshield, and checked the oil for the customer. It was all part of the service.

The young boys and girls worked hard as they grew up and really knew what work was.

When working in the pea fields at harvesting time Bill often drove tractor and cut peas with a sickle mower and picked them up with a hay loader.

He started out with a dollar a week and by the end of the fourth summer he was up to five dollars a week.

He bought his own clothes out of that earned money. Times were hard and money was scarce. Bill worked hard all week, seven days a week with no time for movies or other things that most kids take for granted these days.

If he had any free time it was in the evening, but even then in the summer time there was usually work to do. But Bill didn't mind as he thought a lot of his Aunt Rose and Uncle Everett.

Bill's mother was in good health most of the time and lived to be about seventy six. Though Bill was driving truck at the time, he was in Tennessee when she passed away, but he was able to get home the next day.

Bill's father contracted "TB" and went to the Veterans Hospital where they cured him after three or four years.

At the age of seventy two, Bill's father seem to give up on life but lived to be eighty two. He contracted pneumonia and that was what took him.

Bill wanted to drive truck at eighteen but had to finish high school first. His parents did not want him to drive truck.

At nineteen He joined the Army at the time of the Korean War and was sent to Neuronberg, Germany for twenty seven months. He liked it there and would like to visit it again if it were possible.

He spent four years in the army doing what he could for his country. He is still proud of serving his country as are so many others.

As for myself, I had three brothers in the Army during World War Two. One in during the Korean War and one in during the Vietnam War.

Since then many of my nieces and nephews and so far one grandson has been in either the Marines or the Navy. I am very proud of Bill and the others who have served. Bill's son Mike also served during the Vietnam War.

My first husband "Basil" served in the Army and was also sent to Germany. It seemed to be the place to be sent to.

A year after Bill returned from the Service he got married to his childhood sweetheart where as she had graduated a few months before. She was an only child and as an only child goes, they are usually spoiled.

Bill talked about her being a good cook and a good housekeeper. He and his first wife had four sons which he was and is proud of and he is proud of what the three of them have accomplished in their life time.

I mention three because they lost a newborn son. It left them both devastated.

Whenever Bill mentions Charles Roy he tears up and I want to cry with him.

It is so sad to lose a loved one, no matter how young or old they are. Bill and his first wife were married for twenty eight years.

Being on the road so much, the marriage became rocky and though Bill tried to keep things working, being apart so much just didn't work out.

They had bought a semi-tractor and decided they would try trucking together and Bill looked forward to that. They would be able to spend more time together. His wife could drive semi and that pleased Bill a lot.

But before it could come about, Bill learned she had already found someone else and she asked for a divorce.

He had really tried to make a decent living for her and the family and to make the marriage work. It seems that sometimes it just isn't enough and of course other factors always seem to enter into it.

It's been my theory that a person should not get married right out of high school. Take a year or two to be on your own and do things you really would like to do before you settle down and start a family. Find out who you are first.

From the time you are born, you are under someone else's thumb and you have no idea what it's like to be your own boss and not have someone else tell you what to do. If a person loves you enough they will give you that time and wait for you.

Through hard feelings and losing another son, Bill picked himself up and went back to the thing that would help him recover from his losses.

Having driven truck since nineteen sixty eight and doing other jobs, he knew the truck would be his salvation.

His first trucking job was hauling wall board to the Bunny Club at Lake Geneva, Wisconsin and after that he knew he was hooked on the road. The long distance trips and getting home again to his family was his thrill in life.

Bill was married again a few years later and due to unusual circumstances, he was divorced two years later.

As you know now it was the squeaky cart that led us to each other and made us one.

We are pretty much compatible. It is scary sometimes when we can tell what the other person is thinking. We pretty much like the same things, except I have always been an avid reader of books and he likes the newspapers and magazines.

We both like to watch the NASCAR races. His favorite racer of all times is Mr. Dick Trickle. But today he roots for Matt Kenseth and really gets upset when he doesn't do better. My favorite of course is coming. We both like Kyle Bush and Carl Edwards. I love his back flips and his gorgeous smile and of course his great personality.

The Big Wheel Bug keeps taking a bite out of Bill and we're hoping that soon he will be back on the road again!

It's been an interesting life as a trucker's wife and I wouldn't have missed it for anything.

After living with the bare necessities for six years, it will seem good to set up housekeeping once again and enjoy our children and grandchildren and life as we knew it.

So we say good bye to the eighteen wheelers that took us across the good old United States Of America and presented us with sights unknown.

We thank those who gave us some enlightening stories and friendly chatter on the old C.B.

Perhaps someday, up there on high, we'll know the answer as to why there's no dispatchers in the sky.

18 Wheels and Bill is how we see our country today and the years before.

So much has been lost to all of us and "today we are afraid" our precious freedom will be taken away from us. Our freedom of speech is very precious to us all.

We are seeing T-parties—protestors across our nation. They are only trying to keep what we all want to hold onto.

Yes, we must give some, but must we give all?

This is our country—the U.S. of A. We plan to keep it free for our children, grandchildren and those to come after.

Let freedom ring for all!

So long Friends!!!

This Book is dedicated to my husband Bill who took me across America and made my life so interesting and shared so many stories with me.